Walking Faithfully with God

KAY ARTHUR
BRAD BIRD

HARVEST HOUSE PUBLISHERS

EUGENE, OREGON

All Scripture quotations in this book are taken from the New American Standard Bible®, © 1960, 1962, 1963, 1968, 1971, 1972, 1973, 1975, 1977, 1995 by The Lockman Foundation. Used by permission.

Except where otherwise indicated, all maps and charts in this book, as well as the "How to Get Started" portion of the introductory material, have been adapted and condensed from *The New Inductive Study Bible*, Copyright © 2000 by Precept Ministries International.

Cover by Koechel Peterson & Associates, Minneapolis, Minnesota

The New Inductive Study Series
WALKING FAITHFULLY WITH GOD

Copyright © 1997 by Precept Ministries International
Published by Harvest House Publishers
Eugene, Oregon 97402

Library of Congress Cataloging-in-Publication Data
  Arthur, Kay, 1933-
  [Come walk in my ways]
  Walking faithfully with God / Kay Arthur, Brad Bird.
    p. cm. — (The new inductive study series)
  Originally published: Come walk in my ways. Eugene, Or. : Harvest House Publishers,
    c1997.
  ISBN 0-7369-1386-6 (pbk.)
  1. Bible. O.T. Kings—Study and teaching. 2. Bible. O.T. Chronicles, 2nd—Study and
  teaching. I. Bird, Brad. II. Title.
  BS1335.5.A78 2004
  222'.5'0071—dc22   2003021013

Printed in the United States of America.

04 05 06 07 08 09 10 11 12 / BP-MS / 10 9 8 7 6 5 4 3 2 1

CONTENTS

∾∾∾∾

WHAT AM I DOING?

∾∾∾∾

You are about to begin a study which will revolutionize not only your approach to the Word of God, but also your understanding and comprehension of the Word. This is the consistent testimony of those who are using this series.

The New Inductive Study Series is the first series of its kind in that it is a 15 to 25 minute daily study that takes you systematically through the Bible, book by book, teaching you to observe the text and see for yourself what it says. The more you learn to carefully observe the text and to familiarize yourself with the context in which specific texts are presented, the closer you will come to an accurate and unbiased interpretation of God's Word. This, in turn, will help you correctly apply the truth of God's Word—and find yourself transformed in the process.

As you go through this series, remember that it is an *inductive survey* of the various books of the Bible. The purpose of this series is to help you get a comprehensive overview of the whole counsel of God so that you will be better able to let Scripture interpret Scripture and understand truth in the context of the Bible, book by book and in its entirety.

If you desire to expand and sharpen your study skills, we would like to recommend two things. One, purchase the book *How to Study Your Bible* by Kay Arthur. Two, attend a Precept Ministries Institute of Training.

The Institutes are conducted throughout the United States, Canada, and in a number of other countries. You can attend classes of various lengths—from two hours to five full days, depending on the courses you elect to take. Whatever your choices, you will join the thousands who are absolutely awed at the way God has enriched their relationship to Him and deepened their understanding of His Word. For more information on the Precept Ministries Institute of Training, contact Precept Ministries International at 800-763-8280, visit our website at www.precept.org, or fill out and mail the card at the back of this book.

$\mathcal{H}$OW TO $\mathcal{G}$ET $\mathcal{S}$TARTED...

We don't know if you have ever used one of the books in our New Inductive Study Series before, so let us acknowledge that reading directions is sometimes difficult and hardly ever enjoyable! Most often, you just want to get started. Only if all else fails are you ready to tackle the instructions! We understand—we're not into details either. But read "How to Get Started" before you begin. Believe us, it will help! This is a vital part of getting started on the right foot! The pages are few...and they will help you immensely.

FIRST

As you study the books of 1 and 2 Kings and 2 Chronicles, you will need four things in addition to this book:

1. A Bible you are willing to mark in. Marking is essential because it is an integral part of the learning process and will help you remember and retain what you learn. An ideal Bible for this purpose is *The New Inductive Study Bible (NISB)*. The *NISB* comes in a single-column text format with larger, easy-to-read type, and is ideal for marking. The page margins are wide and blank for note-taking.

The *NISB* also has instructions for studying each book of the Bible, but it does not contain any commentary on the text. The *NISB* isn't compiled from any particular theological stance since its purpose is to teach you how to discern truth for yourself through the inductive method of study.

Inductive Bible study simply means that the Bible itself is one's primary source for study. (The various charts and maps that you will find in this study guide are taken from the *NISB*.) Whatever Bible you use, just know you will need to mark in it, which brings us to the second item you will need.

2. A fine-point, four-color ballpoint pen or various colored fine-point pens (such as Micron pens) for writing in your Bible. The Micron pens are best for this purpose. Office supply stores should have these.

3. Colored pencils or an eight-color Pentel pencil.

4. A composition notebook or loose-leaf notebook for working on your assignments and recording your insights.

SECOND

1. As you study 1 and 2 Kings and 2 Chronicles, you'll find specific instructions for each day's study. The study should take you 15 to 25 minutes a day. However, just know that the more time you can give to this study, the greater the spiritual dividends, the greater your intimacy with the Word of God and the God of the Word. If you are doing this study within the framework of a class and you find the lessons too heavy, simply do what you can. To do a little is better than to do nothing. Don't be an all-or-nothing person when it comes to Bible study.

As a word of warning, you need to be aware that any time you get into the Word of God, you enter into more intensive warfare with the devil (our enemy). Why? Every piece of the Christian's armor is related to the Word of God. And the enemy doesn't want you prepared for battle. Thus, the warfare! Remember that our one and only offensive weapon is the sword of the Spirit, which is the Word of God, and it is enough to fell the enemy.

To study or not to study is a matter of choice first, discipline second. It's a matter of the heart. On what or whom are you setting your heart? Get armed for war! And remember, victory is certain.

2. As you read each chapter, train yourself to think through the content of the text by asking the "5 W's and an H": who, what, when, where, why, and how. Posing questions like these and searching out the answers helps you see exactly what the Word of God is saying. When you interrogate the text with the 5 W's and an H, you ask questions like:

    a. **What** is the chapter about?
    b. **Who** are the main characters?
    c. **When** does this event or teaching take place?
    d. **Where** does this happen?
    e. **Why** is this being done or said?
    f. **How** did this happen?

3. The "when" of events or teachings is very important and should be marked in an easily recognizable way in your Bible. We do this by putting a clock (like the one shown here) in the margin of our Bibles beside the verse where the time phrase occurs. Or you may want to underline references to time in one specific color. As a reminder, note on your key word bookmark (which is explained next in this section) how you are going to mark time references in each chapter.

4. You will be told about certain key words that you should mark throughout this study. This is the purpose of the colored pencils and the colored pen. While this may seem a little time-consuming, you will discover that it is a valuable learning tool. If you develop the habit of marking your Bible, you will find it will make a significant difference

in the effectiveness of your study and in how much you retain as a result of your study.

A **key word** is an important word that is used by the author repeatedly in order to convey his message to his reader. Certain key words will show up throughout the book, while other key words will be concentrated in specific chapters or segments of the book. When you mark a key word, you should also mark its synonyms (words that mean the same thing in the context) and any pronouns *(he, his, she, her, it, we, they, us, our, you, their, them)* in the same way you have marked the key word. Because some people have requested them, we will give you various ideas and suggestions in your daily assignments for how to mark different key words.

Marking words for easy identification can be done by colors, symbols, or a combination of colors and symbols. However, colors are easier to distinguish than symbols. If you use symbols, we suggest you keep them very simple. For example, one of the key words in these books is *Israel.* You could draw a star of David over the word like this: Israel. If a symbol is used in marking a key word, it is best for the symbol to convey the meaning of the word.

When we mark the members of the Godhead (which we do not always mark), we use a triangle to represent the Father, Son, and Holy Spirit. We then color it yellow. Then playing off the triangle we mark the Son this way: Jesus, and the Holy Spirit this way: Spirit . We find that when you mark every reference to God, Jesus, and the Holy Spirit your Bible becomes cluttered. Therefore we suggest you only do this in specific instances. Obviously, since we are studying Old Testament history there will be few references to Jesus or the Holy Spirit. However, you learn much about the Father in the Old Testament. When you gain insight into God's character, power, or ways, you may want to draw a triangle in the margin of the text and record what you learn about Him from that particular text. As you do so, eventually you will form a biblical "theology" about the person of God that will increase your confidence and your faith.

As you begin this new venture, we recommend that you devise a color-coding system for marking key words that you decide to mark throughout your Bible. Then, when you glance at the pages of your Bible, you will have instant recognition of the words.

When you start marking key words, it is easy to forget how you are marking them. Therefore, we recommend you use the bottom portion of the perforated card in the back of this book and write the key words on it. Mark the words in the way you plan to mark them in the Bible text, and then use the card as a bookmark. It might be good to make one bookmark for words you are marking throughout your Bible and a different one for any specific book of the Bible you are studying. Or record your marking system for the words you plan to mark throughout your Bible on a blank page in your Bible.

5. Because locations are important in a historical or biographical book of the Bible (and 1 and 2 Kings and 2 Chronicles are historical books), you will find it helpful to mark locations in a distinguishable way in your study. Try double underlining every reference to a location in green (grass and trees are green!). We suggest that you make a note on your key word bookmark to mark locations. Maps are included in this study so you can look up the locations in order to put yourself into context geographically.

6. Charts called 1 KINGS AT A GLANCE, 2 KINGS AT A GLANCE, and 2 CHRONICLES AT A GLANCE are

located at the end of the book. When you complete your study of each chapter of the book, record the main theme of that chapter on the appropriate chart. A chapter theme is a brief description or summary of the main or predominant subject, teaching, or event covered in that chapter. Usually in historical or biographical books, the chapter themes center around events.

When stating chapter themes, it is best to use words found within the text itself and to be as brief as possible. Make sure that you do it in such a way as to distinguish one chapter from another.

You will record themes on the AT A GLANCE chart. Doing this will help you to remember what each chapter is about. In addition, it will provide you with a ready reference if you desire to find something in the book rather quickly and without a lot of page turning.

If you develop the habit of filling out the AT A GLANCE charts as you progress through the study, you will have a complete synopsis of the book when you finish. If you have *The New Inductive Study Bible,* you will find the same charts in your Bible. If you record your chapter themes on the charts in your Bible, you'll always have them for ready reference.

7. Begin your study with prayer. Don't start without it. Why? Well, although you are doing your part to handle the Word of God accurately, remember that the Bible is a divinely inspired book. The words you are reading are absolute truth, given to you by God so you can know Him and His ways more intimately. These truths are divinely understood:

> For to us God revealed them through the Spirit;
> for the Spirit searches all things, even the depths
> of God. For who among men knows the thoughts

of a man except the spirit of the man which is in him? Even so the thoughts of God no one knows except the Spirit of God (1 Corinthians 2:10,11).

This is why you need to pray. Simply tell God you want to understand His Word so you can live accordingly. Nothing pleases Him more than obedience—honoring Him as God—as you are about to see.

8. Each day, when you finish your lesson, take some time to think about what you read, what you saw with your own eyes. Ask your heavenly Father how you can apply these insights, principles, precepts, and commands to your own life. At times, depending on how God speaks to you through His Word, you might want to record these "Lessons for Life" in the margin of your Bible next to the text you have studied. Simply put "LFL" in the margin of your Bible, then, as briefly as possible, record the lesson for life that you want to remember. You can also make the note "LFL" on your key word bookmark as a reminder to look for these when you study. You will find them encouraging...sometimes convicting...when you come across them again.

THIRD

This study is designed so that you have an assignment for every day of the week. This puts you where you should be—in the Word of God on a daily basis. If you will do your study daily, you will find it more profitable than doing a week's study in one sitting. Pacing yourself this way allows time for thinking through what you learn on a daily basis. However, whatever it takes to get it done, do it!

The seventh day of each week has several features that differ from the other six days. These features are designed to aid in one-on-one discipleship, group discussions, and

Sunday school classes. However, they are also profitable even if you are studying this book by yourself.

The "seventh" day is whatever day in the week you choose to finish your week's study. On this day, you will find a verse or two for you to memorize and STORE IN YOUR HEART. This will help you focus on a major truth or truths covered in your study that week.

To assist those using the material in a Sunday school class or a group Bible study, there are QUESTIONS FOR DISCUSSION OR INDIVIDUAL STUDY. Whatever your situation, seeking to answer these questions will help you reason through some key issues in the study.

If you are using this study in a group setting, make sure the answers given are supported from the Bible text itself. This practice will help ensure that you are handling the Word of God accurately. As you learn to see what the text says, you will find that the Bible explains itself.

Always examine your insights by carefully observing the text to see what it *says*. Then, before you decide what the passage of Scripture *means*, make sure you interpret it in the light of its context. Context is what goes with the text…the Scriptures preceding and following what is written. Scripture will never contradict Scripture. If it ever seems to contradict the rest of the Word of God, you can be certain that something is being taken out of context. If you come to a passage that is difficult to understand, reserve your interpretations for a time when you can study the passage in greater depth.

The purpose of a THOUGHT FOR THE WEEK is to help you apply what you've learned. We've done this for your edification. In this, a little of our theology will inevitably come to the surface; however, we don't ask that you always agree with us. Rather, think through what is said in light of the context of the Word of God. You can determine how valuable it is.

Remember, books in the New Inductive Study Series are survey courses. If you want to do a more in-depth study of a particular book of the Bible, we suggest you do a Precept Upon Precept Bible Study Course on that book. The Precept studies are awesome but require five hours of personal study a week. However, you will never learn more! They are top of the line! You may obtain more information on these courses by contacting Precept Ministries International at 800-763-8280, visiting our website at www.precept.org, or filling out and mailing the response card at the back of this book.

1 KINGS

INTRODUCTION TO
1 KINGS

The book of 1 Kings recounts the history of the kings of Israel from Solomon to Zedekiah. Although the book opens with the great King David sitting on the throne of Israel, the first words of 1 Kings tell us David is nearing the end of his life. Thus, the time had come to anoint another king. Although many vied for the throne, only one could take the seat.

God desired a king who would cling to Him, who would follow Him fully, who would keep His commandments—one who would lead His people in His ways. God's king would be a man after His own heart, even as David was.

God's desire toward you is the same. As the Scripture says, He looks for men and women whose hearts are fully His so that He can strongly support them. That is our desire, our prayer for you as you study the book of 1 Kings. As you observe our God and the greatness of His faithfulness to His people, we pray that your study will deepen your desire to fully walk in His ways.

ℋOW ℭAN ℽOU ℋAVE ℋUCCESS ℰVERY ℋAY ℽOU ℑURN?

ᎧᎧᎧᎧ

Before you begin your study, if you have not read the "How to Get Started" section in the front of this book, it would be beneficial to do so before you go any further. It will explain the method of study we will be using in this book and define the terms we use in the instructions which follow. Next, make a bookmark for your key words in this study from the perforated card in the back of this book as suggested in the "How to Get Started" section. Write the following words on the card and mark or color-code them in the same way you plan to mark them in your Bible: *heart*,[1] *walk*[2]*(ed)*,[3] *pray (prayer, prays, praying, prayed, supplication*[4]*)*, *covenant(ed*[5]*)* (don't mark it when it refers to the ark of the covenant of the Lord), *wisdom*[6] *(wise[r])*, *curse*[7]*(d)*,[8] *command*[9]*(ed)/commandment(s)*[10] *(statutes, ordinances, testimonies)*, *promise*[11]*(d)*,[12] *high place(s)*,[13] *evil (wicked, wickedness)*,[14] *house*[15] (when it refers to the *house of God*), *sin(ned)*,[16] *transgress(ed)*,[17] *Israel*,[18] and *Judah*.[19] Again, as a reminder, be certain to mark in the same way any pronouns or synonyms that refer to each of these words.

As you complete your weekly lessons, there are several exercises that you will want to incorporate into your study times.

First, each day as you read the assigned material, identify and mark the key words that you have been instructed

19

to put on your bookmark. Also mark time phrases, such as numbers of days, years, specific months, and geographical locations.

Second, in some instances you'll want to compile lists on the information you glean from the key words in your notebook to help broaden your understanding of those words. If you compile a list, each day add the insights you see from marking the key words. Leave room in your notebook for your lists.

Third, chart information on each king you study. The chart you will use to record these insights is THE KINGS OF ISRAEL AND JUDAH (pages 121-24). Fill in the king's name, the length of his reign, and any insights you gain about his character and lifestyle.

Finally, begin each day with prayer. Ask God to give you wisdom and insight into the lives of the kings of Israel and Judah so that you might learn practical lessons of life from their lives and God's dealings with them. God has great things in store for you in this study of Kings; be diligent and be willing to allow the Holy Spirit to be your teacher.

As you have noticed, our study covers 1 and 2 Kings and 2 Chronicles. Reading parallel Scriptures will allow you to glean additional information about the kings and the events surrounding this period of Israel's history. As a final note of preparation, be aware that some differences exist in the accounts of events related by the different writers of Kings and Chronicles. The differences in the accounts range from something as simple as the difference in the way the name of a king is spelled to the inclusion of additional details and information surrounding the events. These kinds of differences exist since different authors had different purposes for their writings.

The author of Kings was concerned with the response of each king to the covenant requirements established by

God. The books of 1 and 2 Kings also give accounts of the rulers of both the Northern and Southern kingdoms. The author of 2 Chronicles focuses more on worship and the celebrations that were given to Israel as a safeguard. The Chronicles author highlights in a special way the great moments of trial and victory in the reigns of the great kings of the Southern Kingdom. Therefore, Chronicles often gives details in the lives of the kings of Judah that are not mentioned in Kings. You will want to take notes on any additional information you learn from 2 Chronicles in your notebook.

DAY ONE

Read 1 Kings 1 today and mark any key words you see in the text. Then read it again, marking the time phrases. Note what is happening and when. Also mark in a distinctive way each of the following men: *David, Adonijah,* and *Solomon,* including synonyms (such as *king,* but be careful to check the context to see if it's referring to *David* or *Solomon*) and pronouns (such as *he* or *my*) that refer to each one. Notice what happened when men tried to establish themselves as kings apart from God's plan.

When you have completed your observations of the chapter, record the relevant information on THE KINGS OF ISRAEL AND JUDAH chart beginning on page 121.

If you did the New Inductive Study Series on 1 and 2 Samuel, then you recorded quite a bit of information on David. Should you want to complete the process, it would be good to record all you learn about King David from 1 Kings. You might also want to start compiling a list of all you learn about Solomon from these books. Set aside several pages in your notebook for this list.

Identify and record the theme of chapter 1 on the
1 KINGS AT A GLANCE chart on page 115.

DAY TWO

Read 1 Kings 2 and mark the key words. Note David's
charge to Solomon, and record the outcome of obedience
on your list of insights about Solomon. This charge shows
God's heart for His king and His people. Identify the theme
of chapter 2 and record it on your 1 KINGS AT A GLANCE
chart on page 115.

DAY THREE

First Kings 3 is a wonderful chapter. As you read and
mark the key words, note how Solomon responded when
God said, "Ask what *you wish* me to give you." Take special
note of God's response. Did God answer Solomon's request?
Why? What incident in this chapter gives evidence of God's
decision? Record the answers to these questions on your list
on Solomon. Also read 2 Chronicles 1 and mark the key
words; it is the parallel account of chapter 3 in 1 Kings.

Add to your lists any new insights. Then, after discerning the themes of 1 Kings 3 and 2 Chronicles 1, record
them on the appropriate AT A GLANCE charts on pages
115 and 117, respectively.

DAY FOUR

Read 1 Kings 4–5. Chapter 4 may seem tedious, but
read it carefully. Mark the key words. Then on the map

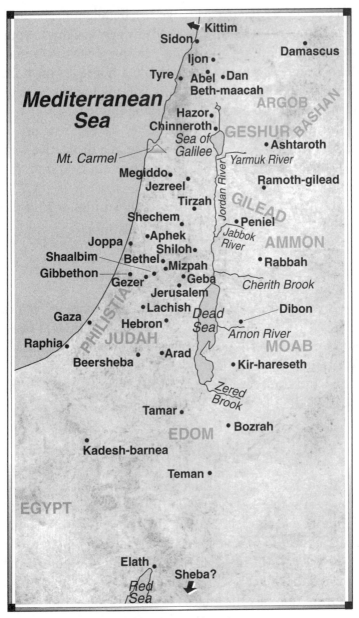

Solomon's Kingdom

SOLOMON'S KINGDOM (page 23), highlight the boundaries that were under his rule. Add any new insights to your lists. As you add to your list on Solomon, be sure to note the reason he was permitted to build a house for the Lord (5:1-6). Since *house* is a key word, you might want to keep a list of what you learn from marking this word.

Go back and read 1 Kings 5:12 to see the certainty of the promises of God. Mark this verse in a distinctive way. List in your notebook what you learn about God from the first five chapters.

Identify and record the themes of 1 Kings 4–5 on the 1 KINGS AT A GLANCE chart on page 115.

DAY FIVE

Read 2 Chronicles 2–3:2 (the parallel passage to 1 Kings 4–5). As you read, mark the key words and time phrases. Add any additional insights about Solomon and your key words to your lists in your notebook.

Identify and record the theme of 2 Chronicles 2 on the 2 CHRONICLES AT A GLANCE chart on page 117.

DAY SIX

Read 1 Kings 6–7. Then read 2 Chronicles 3–5:1. As you mark the key words in these two segments of Scripture, watch especially for any references to time and geographical locations. (When marking references to the *house of the LORD*, don't miss marking the pronouns *it* and *its* when they refer to God's house.) When you finish, note in the margin of your Bible (for easy reference) or in your notebook when the temple (the house) of the Lord was built—when it was begun and when it was completed. As you read, give special attention to 1 Kings 6:11-13. On your list of Solomon, record what he was to do and what God would do if Solomon obeyed. If you do not have *The New Inductive Study Bible* with its illustrations of the temple and its furniture as described in these passages, you will find a drawing of the house of the Lord below.

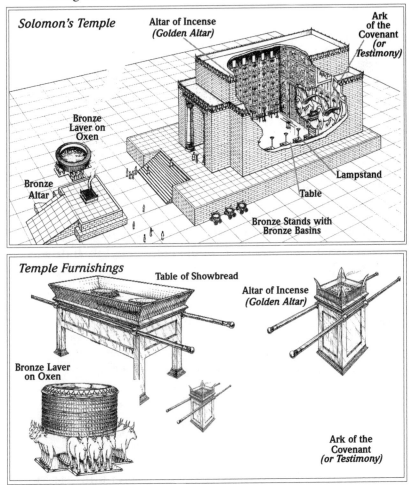

Solomon's Temple and Its Furnishings

Add to your key words lists and list on Solomon. After you discern the themes of 1 Kings 6–7 and 2 Chronicles 3–4, record them on the appropriate AT A GLANCE charts. Also, did you see any "Lessons for Life" (LFLs) in this first week of study? (See page 13 in the "How to Get Started" section.) If so, write them in the margin of your Bible or in your notebook.

DAY SEVEN

Store in your heart: 1 Kings 3:9.
Read and discuss: 1 Kings 2:1-4; 3:1-9; 6:11-13.

QUESTIONS FOR DISCUSSION OR INDIVIDUAL STUDY

1 Kings 2:1-4

ɷ What is the charge given to Solomon from his father, David?

ɷ Discuss what he was told to do with respect to the Word of God and what would happen to him if he was obedient.

1 Kings 3:1-9

ɷ What do you see about Solomon that was different from his father?

ɷ Why did Solomon go to Gibeon?

ɷ What did God ask of Solomon?

ɷ What was Solomon's response?

1 Kings 6:11-13

ɷ Discuss the conditions God gave Solomon in relation to the house of God and the behavior of the children of

Israel. What are the promises God makes in return for obedience?

∾ What principles or precepts did you learn this week from the lives of David and Solomon that you can apply to your own life?

THOUGHT FOR THE WEEK

Solomon was given an incredible responsibility as the new king of Israel. He was to follow in his father's steps, and he was to build a house of the Lord—something no one had been allowed to do. The expectations were high but not impossible. As God had been with David, so He would be with Solomon. Solomon began well. When God gave him the opportunity to make any request of Him, Solomon, recognizing his human impotence, cried for an understanding heart and for the ability to discern between good and evil so that he could properly judge God's people. Pleased with his response, God granted this request, along with many riches. There would be no one like Solomon. First Kings 3:3 tells us, "Now Solomon loved the LORD, walking in the statutes of his father David, except he sacrificed and burned incense on the high places." Solomon compromised in his worship of the Lord. It was a compromise that would lead to others, as you will see. It was a compromise that would eventually divide the nation he wanted to judge wisely.

As you continue your study, tell God that you want to be obedient in all things, not in just some or most. When we begin to compromise, to give in to the smallest of things that this world has to offer, our hearts begin to drift away from our first love. Don't let that happen to you. Don't let that happen to you, beloved of God. You have more than Solomon had. You have the indwelling Holy Spirit.

WHERE IS GOD'S TEMPLE NOW?

As you study the dedication of the house of the Lord this week, you will come across a familiar verse. Second Chronicles 7:14 says, "[If] My people who are called by My name humble themselves and pray and seek My face and turn from their wicked ways, then I will hear from heaven, will forgive their sin and will heal their land." As you study this passage, quoted and claimed by so many Christians today, you will discover the context in which the promise was made. Then you will understand why, in the homes of their dispersion, the Jews marked the wall that faced Jerusalem and faced that way as they prayed to the God who had justly judged them.

May your study this week be used of God to incline your heart to Him that you might walk in His ways and keep His statutes and His ordinances which He has commanded. If you are truly a child of God, your body is His temple and the Spirit never makes us lawless. Rather, He fulfills the righteousness of the law through us! This is holiness.

DAY ONE

First Kings 8 and 2 Chronicles 5:2–7:10 are very important passages. They will be our subject of study for the next three days. Today we want to focus on the general content of 1 Kings 8. Read through the chapter and mark the key words on your bookmark. Also mark the word *cloud*[20] (or *glory* if it refers to the cloud) since it is a key word in this chapter. Now go back and add any pertinent insights to your lists, and make a list of the insights you glean from observing the word *cloud* (or *glory*).

Record the theme of chapter 8 on your 1 KINGS AT A GLANCE chart.

DAY TWO

As you read 1 Kings 8:31-53 yesterday, you might have seen a pattern in the text. Each new paragraph contains the phrase "then hear Thou in heaven." Each time this phrase is used it is preceded by "if" or "when," which sets up a condition in which the children of Israel would someday find themselves. Mark the phrase *then hear in heaven* (or any similar phrase), and note the conditions or circumstances associated with the "if" or "when." Also mark the *ifs* and the *whens*[21] in a distinguishable way.

When you finish your assignment, review what you have marked and note what God has control over.

DAY THREE

Your assignment for today is to read 2 Chronicles 5:2–7:22 and mark the key words. Also mark *then hear* or *then hear from heaven* (or similar phrases), along with every occurrence of *if* and *when* (when used with these phrases).

Now do you see the setting of 2 Chronicles 7:14? Does the context and all that you observed these past three days shed greater light on your understanding of this verse we so often quote and claim? Did you notice the inclusion of the "foreigner" or "stranger" in 1 Kings 8:41-43 and 2 Chronicles 6:32,33? Interesting, isn't it!

Identify and record the theme of 2 Chronicles 5–7 on the 2 CHRONICLES AT A GLANCE chart. Also add any new insights to your lists.

DAY FOUR

Read 1 Kings 9. Mark key words and time references. In 9:1-9 take careful note of what the Lord did, what He required from Solomon and the sons of Israel, and the consequences of obedience or disobedience. Take careful notes of what you learn from marking the references to the *house of the LORD* in this chapter.

Make pertinent notes on your key word lists in your notebook, and identify and record the theme of 1 Kings 9 on the 1 KINGS AT A GLANCE chart.

DAY FIVE

Your assignment for today is to read 2 Chronicles 7:11–8:18 to get a more complete historical picture of the events you studied in Kings yesterday. (We realize you have already read through chapter 7; however, we want you to see the chronological parallels with 1 Kings 9.)

Watch for the two different spellings of the name of the king of Tyre. In Kings his name is spelled *Hiram*, but it is spelled *Huram* in Chronicles.[22]

Identify and record the theme of 2 Chronicles 8 on the 2 CHRONICLES AT A GLANCE chart.

DAY SIX

Today read 1 Kings 10, marking key words. In this passage, the reader is introduced to the Queen of Sheba. Note what you learn about her as you seek out the answers to the 5 W's and an H: who, what, when, where, why, and how (see "How to Get Started," page 9).

When you finish, record in your notebook the ways God blessed Solomon, and add any new information to your lists.

Now read 2 Chronicles 9, the parallel passage for 1 Kings 10. Identify the chapter themes and record them on the appropriate charts. (At this point in your study this should be part of your daily routine; therefore, we won't keep repeating the instruction to record the chapter themes except to occasionally remind you of this process.)

Did you see any LFLs in this week's homework that you can apply to your life? If so, make a note of them in your notebook or Bible.

DAY SEVEN

Store in your heart: 2 Chronicles 7:13,14. If you have already memorized these verses, then memorize 1 Kings 8:23 or 8:61.

Read and discuss: 1 Kings 8:22-61; 2 Chronicles 6–7. (Read these segments as you come to them in your discussion.)

QUESTIONS FOR DISCUSSION OR INDIVIDUAL STUDY

∾ As you studied 1 Kings 8 and 2 Chronicles 6–7, what did you learn about God? (If you are doing this in a group study, having a board to write on would be helpful so you can list the insights of the class members, along with the verses which gave them their perceptions.)

∾ How will such knowledge of God help you in your day-to-day affairs?

∾ What did you learn from marking the references to *if* or *when* and *then hear from (in) heaven?*

∾ What did these verses tell you about God and the realm of His power?

∾ What did you learn about sin, obedience, forgiveness, and the judgment of God?

∾ In Solomon's blessing of the assembly in 1 Kings 8:54-61, what was his desire? Was he taking hold of the charge given him by his father in 1 Kings 2:1-4?

The Temple

∾ What did you learn about the temple? When was it built? How long did it take? What was it like? Where was it located? On whose land?

∾ What did you learn about the Israelites and the ramifications of their obedience or disobedience with respect to the land and the temple?

∾ Do you see any evidence of the impact of these words on the nation of Israel today?*

∾ Today, what is standing where the temple once stood? To whom does that threshing floor where Solomon built the temple belong (2 Chronicles 3:1)? Do you know why the temple no longer stands? According to what you have seen in the Word of God this week, what should the children of Israel be doing?

---

* Kay Arthur has written a bestselling historical and prophetic novel that takes you through every major event of Israel's history from 605 B.C. to the fulfillment of Zechariah 14. Described as "the story of the nation of Israel like no other...in a novel like no other," *Israel, My Beloved* paints a very descriptive picture of the fulfillment of Scripture.

∾ What did you learn this week about the importance of prayer, of communion with God? Did you learn: what things you should pray for? possible physical positions for prayer? how God responds to your prayers?

∾ What was the most significant truth you learned this week that you can apply to your life? Or, to put it another way, what lessons for life have you learned this week? Will they bring any changes to the way you live? If you are in a discussion group, discuss this together.

THOUGHT FOR THE WEEK

As David neared death, he did all he could to assure that Solomon would rule after him. God's desire was a king who would walk in His ways and keep His commandments so He might bless His people. Yet the blessings were not without restrictions: Obedience was the key. And it remains so today. A holy God cannot overlook sin; yet, He makes provision for it by granting forgiveness and merciful favor to those who humble themselves, pray, seek His face, and turn from their wicked ways. As it was then, so it is today. God's desire is for His people to obey Him so that all the people of the earth might know that only one is God. There is no other. (See 1 Kings 8:59-61.)

Are you heeding His call to walk in His ways and obey Him? Is there anything you need to change so your life lines up with His commandments? Ask God to search your heart and reveal that which is displeasing to Him (Psalm 139:23,24). And remember as you go about your day-by-day living, if you are His child, your body is His temple. May everything in His temple say, "Glory."

Whose Influence Are You Following?

Understanding the history of Israel is critical to a full understanding of Scripture as a whole. You are in the process of building a historical and biblical base upon which you can stand. Be diligent to build well, Beloved. Remember each day to go to the Lord in prayer, asking for His wisdom as you study. Pray that He will open your eyes so that you might understand truth. Also pray that He will use this study to not only give you a deeper understanding of the contents of 1 and 2 Kings and 2 Chronicles, but also to help you become more like Christ.

DAY ONE

Read 1 Kings 11, marking the text as you go. This is a very significant chapter because it marks a turn in the course of events. Watch what happens to Solomon in this chapter, then record it on your notebook list.

The following insight box highlights some of the gods introduced to Israel by Solomon's wives. You'll find it enlightening.

Jeroboam is a very important character. Give careful attention to what you learn about him. Once again ask the

35

INSIGHT

Religious Influences of Solomon's Wives

1. Ashtoreth—Sidonian (Canaanite) goddess of fertility, love, and war. Later she became the spouse of Baal (2 Kings 23:13).

2. Milcom—Ammonite god whose name means "king." At the request of his pagan wives, Solomon built sanctuaries to Milcom on the Mount of Olives (2 Kings 23:13).

*3. Chemosh—god of Moab—*meaning "to subdue." Solomon erected a sanctuary for Chemosh on a mountain east of Jerusalem (2 Kings 23:13; Jeremiah 48:7,13,46).

*4. Molech—*a pagan god from Ammon to whom human sacrifices, usually children, were made. This practice was condemned by God (Leviticus 18:21; 20:3-5; 2 Kings 23:10; Jeremiah 32:35). Compare with 2 Kings 17:31 and Jeremiah 7:31; 19:5.

5 W's and an H as you read about him. If you have time, list the insights you discover.

On the chart THE KINGS OF ISRAEL AND JUDAH on pages 121-24, record any new insights on Solomon. Don't forget to record the chapter themes this week.

DAY TWO

Read 1 Kings 12, marking the key words. Give careful attention to Jeroboam and Rehoboam, for they are very significant in the history of Israel. Note the difference between the two men in your notebook. Watch their actions and the consequences of their behaviors and decisions. Romans 15:4 tells us that "whatever was written in earlier times was written for our instruction, so that through perseverance and the encouragement of the Scriptures we might have hope." Therefore it is wisdom to stop and think about what we have observed and how the insights gleaned about these two men can be applied to our daily lives. Record pertinent information on these kings on THE KINGS OF ISRAEL AND JUDAH chart.

In 1 Kings 12:30,31 there is a reference to worship being conducted in the high places. The high places were areas where the people worshiped Baal and other gods. Israel was forbidden to allow such practices when they entered the land of promise. God told them to "drive out all the inhabitants of the land from before you, and destroy all their figured stones, and destroy all their molten images and demolish all their high places" (Numbers 33:52).

Note the events that take place in 1 Kings 12:16-20. The chart entitled ISRAEL'S DIVISION AND CAPTIVITY (below) will give you a good perspective of the division of the kingdom.

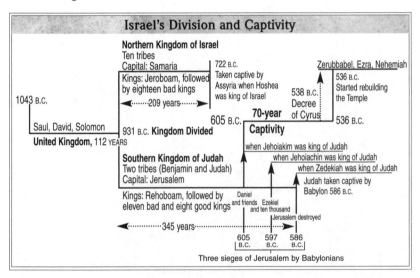

Israel's Division and Captivity

Northern Kingdom of Israel
Ten tribes
Capital: Samaria

Kings: Jeroboam, followed by eighteen bad kings

722 B.C. Taken captive by Assyria when Hoshea was king of Israel

Zerubbabel, Ezra, Nehemiah
536 B.C. Started rebuilding the Temple

538 B.C. Decree of Cyrus

536 B.C.

1043 B.C.

Saul, David, Solomon
United Kingdom, 112 YEARS

◄······209 years······►

605 B.C.

70-year

931 B.C. **Kingdom Divided**

Captivity

when Jehoiakim was king of Judah

when Jehoiachin was king of Judah

when Zedekiah was king of Judah

Judah taken captive by Babylon 586 B.C.

Southern Kingdom of Judah
Two tribes (Benjamin and Judah)
Capital: Jerusalem

Kings: Rehoboam, followed by eleven bad and eight good kings

Daniel and friends   Ezekiel and ten thousand

Jerusalem destroyed

◄············345 years············►

605 B.C. | 597 B.C. | 586 B.C.

Three sieges of Jerusalem by Babylonians

Record the theme of 1 Kings 12. As the kingdom divides, note the boundaries. Refer to the map THE DIVIDED KINGDOM (following page) to get a picture of the separation.

DAY THREE

Read 2 Chronicles 10–11:4, marking key words as you go. This is a parallel account to 1 Kings 12. Look for

Tyre

Dan

Hazor

**Mediterranean
Sea**

Sea of
Galilee

Megiddo

Jezreel

Samaria

Shechem

ISRAEL

River Jordan

Cities of
worship:
Dan
Bethel
Jerusalem

Joppa

Aphek

Gezer

Bethel

Jerusalem

JUDAH

Dead
Sea

Lachish

Gaza   Hebron

*The Divided Kingdom
931-586 B.C.*

additional insights on Jeroboam and Rehoboam. These chapters are very significant in the history of Israel. It would be beneficial to review 1 Kings 12 as you study these chapters in 2 Chronicles.

DAY FOUR

Read 1 Kings 13. Mark key words and time references. Watch the interchange between Jeroboam and the man of God. As you read, list what you learn about the man from Judah who cried against the altar. Note the consequences of his disobedience later in the chapter. Partial obedience is still disobedience.

DAY FIVE

Read and mark 1 Kings 14.

First Kings 14:23 refers to the "Asherim" the children of Israel had made for themselves on every high hill and beneath every luxuriant tree to worship Ashtoreth, the goddess of the Sidonians. These images were associated with the worship of Baal. According to their mythology, Ashtoreth was the wife of Baal.

Give special attention to the fate of Jeroboam and the Northern Kingdom and the reason for it all. Then note what transpired in the Southern Kingdom.

Chart the information on Jeroboam and Rehoboam on THE KINGS OF ISRAEL AND JUDAH chart on pages 121-24. Make a note of what happens to Rehoboam at the end of 1 Kings 14.

DAY SIX

Read 2 Chronicles 11:5–12:16, the parallel account of 1 Kings 14. Mark the key words. Look for additional insights you can glean regarding Jeroboam and Rehoboam, and add them to your chart.

Look carefully at 2 Chronicles 12:7,8. The Lord is compassionate to those who humble themselves; yet, He is still just. Sin cannot go unpunished!

Don't forget to record the themes of 2 Chronicles 11 and 12 on the 2 CHRONICLES AT A GLANCE chart. Make sure these charts are up-to-date with respect to the chapters we have covered.

What LFLs can you focus on this week? Write them out.

DAY SEVEN

Store in your heart: Psalm 119:1-3.
Read and discuss: 1 Kings 11.

QUESTIONS FOR DISCUSSION OR INDIVIDUAL STUDY

∞ Solomon started out strong, committed unwaveringly to God. What happened?

a. Do you think Solomon expected this to happen?

b. What were the consequences?

∞ Discuss the root problem that caused Solomon's downward slide (1 Kings 11:4).

∞ Discuss how God fulfilled His promise to Solomon as written in 1 Kings 11:11-13.

∾ Have you ever known someone who started out on fire for God but whose fire diminished to merely hot embers through the years?

∾ Why do you think loss of commitment occurs?

∾ How did the actions of Solomon affect the future of Israel?

 a. What does this tell you about God?

 b. How does this measure up with what you've learned about God to this point in your study?

∾ If Solomon had obeyed the commandments of the Lord, would the kingdom have divided?

∾ What could Solomon have done to prevent this division (1 Kings 2:1-4)? Each king who came to power was required to write out a copy of the law. Read Deuteronomy 17:14-20 and note what Solomon knew to do, yet he chose not to.

∾ Are you, as Solomon, called to walk in the ways of the Lord? Do you think God will exempt you from what He held Solomon accountable for? Can you give a biblical reason for your answer?

THOUGHT FOR THE WEEK

Solomon was a wise man who certainly knew the truth, yet he chose to walk his own way. In the pursuit of pleasure, in the satisfaction of his desires, he disobeyed God. He sowed to the wind . . . and reaped a whirlwind. The result of his disobedience was the division of Solomon's kingdom into the Northern Kingdom of Israel and the Southern Kingdom of Judah. Perhaps Solomon forgot that the wealth and wisdom he possessed had all come from God. Or did he think that because he built the temple, because he was wise and wealthy, he was exempt from total obedience and the consequences of disobedience?

David had instructed his son Solomon to obey God's commandments, ordinances, and testimonies, and to walk in His ways. If Solomon had listened to his father, if he had followed God without compromise, then he would have succeeded in everything he set his hand to, and his kingdom would have stayed intact. But he didn't listen. His heart turned from the Lord. Beloved, do you see that this same principle applies to us? If our hearts are fully His, if we will walk by the Word of the Lord—rather than be influenced by the world—we will be successful in the things of the Lord. In the midst of your pursuits, may you be ever mindful of the fact that everything you are and all you have are gifts from God. He alone deserves your allegiance. He alone is worthy of your pursuit. Keep your eyes on Him.

Thank God today for how He has made you: for the talents and abilities He has woven into who you are and for the spiritual gifts He gave you when He saved you. Then ask Him if there are things you are holding onto that keep Him from being able to do more in you and through you. Are there people in your life who are influencing you to compromise your walk with and your relationship to God? If so, are you willing to let go of whatever could distract you from wholehearted devotion to the One who alone is worthy of it?

*H*OW *L*ONG-*S*UFFERING *I*S *G*OD IN THE *F*ACE OF THE *D*ISOBEDIENCE OF *H*IS *P*EOPLE?

Solomon and David were dead. The kingdom that was once strong and united was now ripped apart because of Solomon's worldly pursuits. Instead of one king ruling God's people, now there were two. Golden calves were now credited with delivering God's people from their enemies. What a tragedy!

God's people strayed into disobedience, but He remained ever the same, righteous in all His ways, yet ever patient and long-suffering...wholly God! This is the God you serve.

As you study this week, our prayer for you and for ourselves is that we will allow nothing to come between us and our God. As you commit yourself to another week of study, ask God to teach you His character and His ways...which remain consistent throughout eternity.

DAY ONE

Your assignment today is to read 1 Kings 15 and mark the key words. As you read, use two different colors to color-code the descriptions of each king: one color for the evil kings and another color for those who are righteous kings. Also assign a color for each of the kingdoms, and underline each king according to the color of his kingdom, Northern or Southern.

If you have a *New Inductive Study Bible*, you might want to use the same color-code used on the full-color charts of the history of Israel that start on page 42 in the front of the Bible. These charts will not only give you a chronology of the various kings of both kingdoms, but they are designed to help you see the relationship of these kings to each other. They also show the prophets who lived and ministered during the reigns of these kings. If you do not have an *NISB*, black-and-white charts are provided on pages 118-20.

From this point on in your study, once you observe the life of each king from start to finish, record the information on the chart beginning on page 121 as you have been doing. (This chart is also in the *NISB* after 2 Kings. If you have this Bible, you will want to record the information there also.) When you fill in the chart, use the same color-coding you used in your Bible to show whether the king was good or evil. Doing this will help you see the ratio of good kings to evil kings. Note that *Abijam* is spelled *Abijah* in 2 Chronicles (chapter 13). It is interesting to realize that even though Abijam was wicked, God gave him "a lamp in Jerusalem, to raise up his son after him and to establish Jerusalem; because David did what was right in the sight of the LORD, and had not turned aside from anything that He commanded him all the days of his life, except in the case of Uriah the Hittite" (1 Kings 15:4,5).

A prophecy was given in 1 Kings 14:7-16. Its fulfillment is in 1 Kings 15:29,30. You might want to write this cross-reference in the margin of your Bible as a Lesson for Life (LFL): When God says something, He stands by His Word!

Identify and record the theme of 1 Kings 15 on the
1 KINGS AT A GLANCE chart on page 115, and add any
new insights to your key words lists.

DAY TWO

Read 2 Chronicles 13–16:14, continuing to mark key
words. As you did in 1 Kings, color-code the description of
the lifestyle of each king—whether he was wicked or righteous and if he was a king of Israel or a king of Judah.
Although there are many parallel events in these chapters,
be careful to look for new insights. Also record your
themes for chapters 13–15 of 2 Chronicles, and add
insights to your notebook lists of key words.

DAY THREE

Read 1 Kings 16. Mark the key words listed on your
bookmark and add to your lists. Remember to mark the
different kings as you read, employing the coloring system
you devised to denote which kingdom the king reigned
over and whether the king was righteous or wicked. Fill in
information on Baasha, Asa, Elah, Zimri, Omri, and Ahab
on THE KINGS OF ISRAEL AND JUDAH chart. This
chart should be beneficial as you put the book of 1 Kings
together historically.

Note the prophecy given to Jehu concerning Baasha,
along with its fulfillment. The completion of this prophecy
serves as evidence of the sureness of God's Word. Also, note
the fulfillment in verse 34 of the prophecy given by
Joshua (Joshua 6:26). Even though it may be many years

later—even centuries or millennia—you can be certain that what God says will come to pass!

DAY FOUR

Read 1 Kings 17. Mark the key words, time phrases, and geographical locations. Elijah, a significant Bible character, comes on the scene in this chapter. It would be helpful to keep a record in your notebook of the pertinent things you observe about him, his life, and his ministry. Specifically, note the miracles which take place through him. Note Elijah's first words when he comes on the scene of Israel's history. What an introduction!

DAY FIVE

Read 1 Kings 18—a story you may have heard as a child if you went to church. Mark the key words and time phrases. Record additional insights you glean regarding Elijah in your notebook.

Note how God answers Elijah and the miracles God performs through him. Add any new insights to your key words lists.

DAY SIX

Read and mark 1 Kings 19. Update your notes on Elijah. Isn't it interesting that Elijah runs from Jezebel after the miraculous things he has just seen God do! This reminds us that Elijah was a man with a nature like ours; yet, when he earnestly prayed, God listened (see James 5:17,18).

Are you remembering to record the themes of these books? Record the 1 Kings 19 theme on the appropriate chart. Also record what God is showing you for your life through this study.

DAY SEVEN

Store in your heart: 1 Kings 18:21.
Read and discuss: 1 Kings 18.

QUESTIONS FOR DISCUSSION OR INDIVIDUAL STUDY

- When did the Word of the Lord come to Elijah in 1 Kings 18? What was the message?

- What did you learn about Obadiah? Why didn't he want to deliver Elijah's message to King Ahab?

- King Ahab called Elijah the troubler of Israel. Who was the real troubler of Israel? How do you know this?

- Elijah challenges the idolaters to determine whose god will send down fire to prove there is only one true God. What happened?

- What happened when 450 of Baal's prophets cried out to Baal? Why do you think that was?

- Why did Elijah want God to answer him in regard to the confrontation with the servants of Baal? Was it for Elijah's glory or God's glory?

- Why did Elijah place twelve stones around the altar?

- Why did Elijah pour water on the wood for the burnt offering and fill the trench around the altar with water?

∾ When Elijah called on God, why did he ask God to bring down fire?

∾ Was Elijah's prayer answered?

∾ What happened to the prophets of Baal?

∾ What did you learn about God from this chapter?

∾ What did you learn about prayer from this chapter?

∾ What did you see that you could apply to your life from this chapter?

If you're doing this in a group, and there is time, discuss Elijah's flight from Jezebel and the events which immediately follow this account in 1 Kings 19.

THOUGHT FOR THE WEEK

When Elijah set up the challenge between God and Baal, he understood that there really was no challenge. Israel had placed its faith in gods who didn't exist, while the one true God was being rejected. As a result of this confrontation, after God consumed the wood and the ox, the people fell on their faces and said, "The LORD, He is God; the LORD, He is God" (1 Kings 18:39). For one brief moment, God received the acknowledgment due him.

Do you truly recognize that the Lord, He is God? Do you understand just who and what He is? Do you give Him the recognition He deserves? He is a consuming fire with whom we are to be consumed.

As you spend time in His Word this week, may you be consumed with a desire to know Him even more intimately...that you, a man or woman of like passions, might live as Elijah did—holding God to His Word as you communicate with Him in fervent prayer.

ARE YOU PREPARED TO FIGHT BY GOD'S RULES FOR WARFARE?

The Christian life is not without conflict. We are in a spiritual war. The question is, When the battle comes, are you prepared to do battle according to God's rules for warfare?

As Israel and Judah's relationship with God regressed under the leadership of the wicked kings, the battles did not lessen. In most battles, God laid out the plan for success, yet many times His plans were followed only partially, which brings us to the point of application: Are you following God fully, or are you wavering between His plans and your own?

As you study this week, remember that these things are recorded that we might learn by Israel's example.

DAY ONE

Read 1 Kings 20 to familiarize yourself with the chapter. Read it again, marking the key words and references to time. Then read 1 Kings 15:16-22 for a brief refresher on Ben-hadad.

Why did God offer to deliver Ahab from Ben-hadad (1 Kings 20:13)? Give attention to the key events of the battles and the numbers killed in verses 15-30. (You may want to take notes in your notebook on this.) Even through all the sin and disobedience, God never abandoned His people.

After God told Ahab He would destroy Ben-hadad, Ahab made a covenant with Ben-hadad and spared his life. Remembering the covenant between David and Jonathan, how binding was this agreement? Ahab and Ben-hadad were now obligated to defend one another. Think about that for a moment: Ahab made a covenant with a man God had told him to kill! What was the consequence of this decision (1 Kings 20:42)?

Identify and record the theme of chapter 20 on the appropriate chart.

DAY TWO

Read 1 Kings 21 today, marking the key words. Record any fresh insights on Elijah in your notebook, as well as new information you are compiling on specific key words. Carefully read about Ahab and Jezebel's dealings with Naboth and his property. Remember this happens just after God tells Ahab he will lose his life. Did he have a wholesome fear of God at this point in his life?

Did you notice that Jezebel had Ahab call a "fast" concerning the vineyard with Naboth? In Old Testament times, fasts were normally religious in nature and called in times of mourning, trouble, repentance, or in honor of commemorative days. Yet, in an incredible misuse of a religious practice, Jezebel's fast was declared for the purpose of deception and murder!

Mark the prophecy concerning Ahab and Jezebel's deaths, since this notation will be helpful later (1 Kings 21:17-24). Don't miss Ahab's reaction to Elijah's prophecy in 1 Kings 21:27-29. Note in your notebook what you learn about God in these verses.

DAY THREE

Read 1 Kings 22. Mark key words and time references as you study. Remember to color-code the kings so you will know if they were evil or good. Also note their kingdoms and their characters. In this chapter, you are introduced to another interesting prophet: Micaiah. Record any interesting insights you gain about him in your notebook.

Throughout all the events and the different prophecies that have been made, you see that the word of the Lord comes to pass just as He said it would. Read 1 Kings 22:17, then 1 Kings 22:34-36. Look for the similarities between these passages.

In the margin of your Bible, note the fulfillment of the prophecy concerning Ahab's death (22:37,38). Compare 1 Kings 22:37,38 with 1 Kings 21:19. Don't forget to fill out the information on Ahab and Jehoshaphat on THE KINGS OF ISRAEL AND JUDAH chart. Also add the themes for these chapters to their respective AT A GLANCE charts.

DAY FOUR

Today read 2 Chronicles 17 to gain further insight into the life of Jehoshaphat. Then read 2 Chronicles 18, which parallels the events in 1 Kings 22. Watch for additional insights on Jehoshaphat and the battle at Ramoth-gilead. Remember to mark key words, time phrases, and geographical locations. Add new insights to your lists, and put additional insights about Jehoshaphat on THE KINGS OF ISRAEL AND JUDAH chart.

DAY FIVE

Your assignment today is to read 2 Chronicles 19 and mark the key words. Look for additional insights into the life of Jehoshaphat and write them on your chart. In verses 5-7, Jehoshaphat appointed judges. Notice what he instructed them to do and how he instructed them to render judgment. Also, in verses 8-11, Jehoshaphat appointed some of the Levites and priests for judgment. Note Jehoshaphat's relationship to the Lord and how it compared to that of his father, Asa.

DAY SIX

Read 2 Chronicles 20 and mark the key words. Search out the answers to the 5 W's and an H as you read. As you study this chapter, carefully observe the way Jehoshaphat sought the Lord. Watch the content of his prayer and how God responded. Remember to chart the information on Jehoshaphat on the chart on page 121, and add new information to your key words lists.

Record the theme of 2 Chronicles 20 on the AT A GLANCE chart.

DAY SEVEN

Store in your heart: 2 Chronicles 20:17.
Read and discuss: 2 Chronicles 20.

QUESTIONS FOR DISCUSSION OR INDIVIDUAL STUDY

∾ What did Jehoshaphat do when he heard that an enemy was coming against him? Discuss all you observe about his response—from what he experienced to what he called others to do (20:1-4).

∞ Discuss the content of Jehoshaphat's prayer. How did he begin? What did he remind God of? What did he ask God to do? On what basis (20:5-13)?

∞ How do you react when you are faced with a sudden threat from an enemy? What did you learn from Jehoshaphat that you can apply to your own life? How?

∞ How did God respond to Jehoshaphat? What were the Lord's specific instructions to him?

∞ Why do you think God responds as He does?

∞ Were Jehoshaphat and his people fighting their own battle?

∞ What were God's instructions?

∞ Is there anything you can learn from God's response to Jehoshaphat's situation that you can apply to your own life?

∞ What happened when the two armies met?

∞ Did it surprise you to read 2 Chronicles 20:35-37? Discuss what you can learn from this passage that you can apply to your own life.

∞ What have you learned this week about fighting the devil, our enemy, God's way? What should be your battle strategy when you find yourself in spiritual warfare?

∞ What was the most significant truth you learned this week? Why? Is this an LFL you want to write down and remember?

Thought for the Week

Even though Israel made many mistakes during the period of the kings, there were many times they realized that their only hope was in the strength of the Lord. It was in those times that God took it upon Himself to fight their battles for them. Most of their failures came when they tried to fight on their own or play by their own rules.

The same is true today. Perhaps our battles are of a different nature than those of Israel, yet we do face fights every day. It is God's desire that, when we encounter conflict, we turn to Him for wisdom, strength, and direction. Don't make the same mistakes as Israel. Rather, like Jehoshaphat, cast yourself upon the Lord. Trust Him. Remind Him of His promises, seek His direction and leadership, and you will find Him coming to your aid as the captain of the hosts, ready to lead you in the sure victory of faith.

2 KINGS

INTRODUCTION TO 2 KINGS

∾∾∾∾

As you move into the book of 2 Kings, remember that it is a continuation of 1 Kings. By now the truth concisely stated in Daniel 2:21 has become evident: It is God alone who sets kings upon their thrones and who removes them. Sadly, God's desire for faithful, obedient kings—kings who were men after His heart—was rarely fulfilled. Most of Israel and Judah's kings served other gods, followed their own hearts, and, as a result, died in their sins. Although they were unfaithful, God never changed or altered. He remained, and remains today, a loving and compassionate God, righteous and just, always faithful to His Word and to His character.

It is our prayer that you will learn much about God and His ways that you can apply to your life in a very practical, life-changing way.

WHEN GOD SPEAKS, IT WILL BE "ACCORDING TO THE WORD OF THE LORD"

DAY ONE

Remember, student of the Word of God, the revelation of spiritual truth comes from God. Begin each day's study in that attitude of prayerful dependence as you carefully observe God's Word.*

As you study the book of 2 Kings, add the following key phrase to the bookmark[23] you used for 1 Kings: *according to the word of the LORD*.[24] Read 2 Kings 1 and mark key words (including their synonyms and pronouns). Don't forget to mark the time phrases and geographical locations throughout 2 Kings. Add any new insights to your key words lists.

Note the name of the god King Ahaziah called upon in the first few verses of this chapter. Look at the chart on page 59 and see what you learn about this god. Because you will encounter many pagan gods in 2 Kings, it would be good to review this chart in full. It gives you a brief summary of the gods and what they represented to the people who worshiped them.

---

* If you are new to this study, please read the "How to Get Started" section in the front of this book. The information there will help you understand the brief instructions within the study.

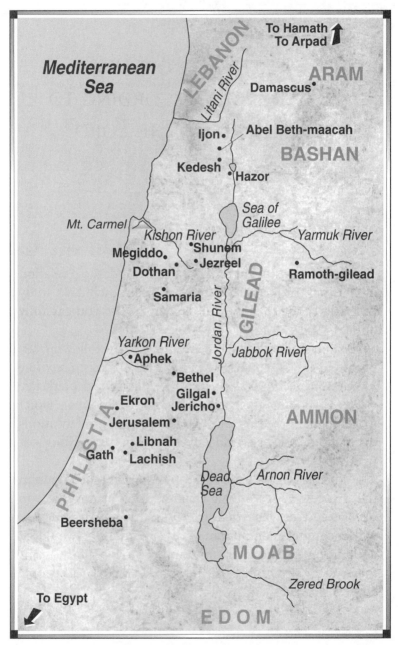

Cities and Geography of 2 Kings

Some of the Pagan Gods Worshiped by the Israelites		
The god:	Ruled over / description:	Reference:
Adrammelech	War, love	2 Kings 17:31
Anammelech	Demanded child sacrifice	2 Kings 17:31
Asherah	Wife of Baal	2 Kings 13:6
Ashima	God of Hittites	2 Kings 17:30
Ashtoreth (Astarte, Ishtar)	Sex, fertility, queen of heaven	2 Kings 23:13
Baal	Rain, wind, clouds, fertility of land	2 Kings 3:2
Baal-zebub	God of Ekron	2 Kings 1:2
Chemosh	Provider of land	2 Kings 23:13
Molech (Milcom)	National god of Moabites, worship involved human sacrifice	2 Kings 23:10
Nebo	Wisdom, literature, arts	1 Chronicles 5:8
Nergal	Underworld, death	2 Kings 17:30
Nibhaz	Worshiped by the Avvites (a people transplanted to Samaria from Assyria)	2 Kings 17:31
Nisroch	God worshiped in Nineveh	2 Kings 19:37
Rimmon	Thunder, lightning, rain	2 Kings 5:18
Succoth-Benoth	Mistress of Marduk, goddess of war	2 Kings 17:30
Tartak	Fertility (worshiped by Avvites)	2 Kings 17:31

In a specific way, mark the prophecy concerning Aha-ziah and the fulfillment of that prophecy.

When you finish reading 2 Kings 1, record what you learn about King Ahaziah on the KINGS OF ISRAEL AND JUDAH chart. Also record what you learn from this chapter about Jehoram, king of Israel. Don't forget to color-code whether he is a good or evil king and which kingdom he is part of.

Add any new insights you gain about Elijah, the prophet of God, to the notes you are keeping in your notebook. Consult the ELIJAH'S MINISTRY map on the following page, which shows where the major events of his ministry occurred.

Identify and record the theme of 2 Kings 1 on your 2 KINGS AT A GLANCE chart on page 116.

DAY TWO

Today's reading is very interesting. As you read chapter 2, you are going to learn more about Elisha, whom you first

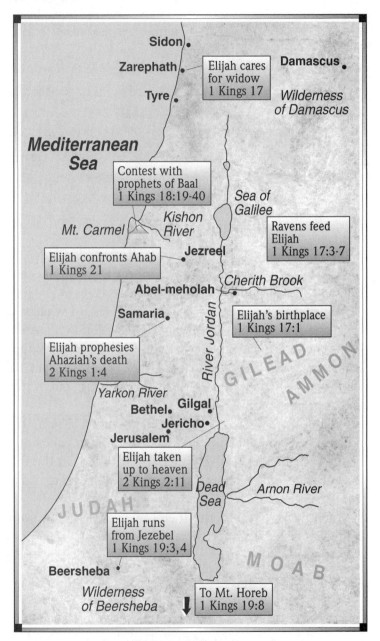

Elijah's Ministry

encountered in 1 Kings 19:16. Study this chapter carefully, observing not only the course of events, but also Elisha's relationship to Elijah. Mark key words and add insights to your lists. You will also want to begin building a list on Elisha.

As you do, make sure you include what you learned from 1 Kings 19:15-21.

DAY THREE

Read 2 Kings 3 and mark the key words. Although 1 Kings 22 tells of the death of Jehoshaphat, this chapter tells of another event in his life.

Note the command Elisha gives the king of Israel in 2 Kings 3:19. Watch to see if the Israelites obey this instruction. Add insights you gleaned regarding Jehoram to the chart about the kings. Also mark *Jehoram* according to your coloring system, to show if he is good or evil and which kingdom he belongs to.

After discerning the theme of chapter 3, record it on the appropriate chart, and add to your key words lists.

DAY FOUR

Read 2 Kings 4. Mark the key words and the key phrase, *according to the word of the LORD*. Continue your list on Elisha; keep it up-to-date.

Read 2 Kings 2:7-14 again, noting the request that Elisha made of Elijah before he was taken up. Is there any evidence that God honored Elisha's request? Note it on your Elisha list.

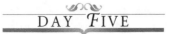

DAY FIVE

Read 2 Kings 5:1-14. Mark the key words. Add the miracles God performs through Elisha to the data you are collecting on him.

Note what Naaman had to learn in order to be healed. When Elisha gave instructions to Naaman, was it what Naaman wanted to hear? Although Naaman didn't like the process, the outcome was exactly what he requested.

Like Naaman, have you ever prayed for a request and received it—yet it wasn't the way you had pictured God working? How did you feel? Can you relate to Naaman?

DAY SIX

Your assignment today is to read 2 Kings 5:15-27 and mark the key words. If you have time, it would be helpful if you reread the first half of the chapter to keep everything in context. Add fresh insights to any lists you are keeping on various key words.

Observe how Gehazi tries to deceive Naaman and Elisha for his own benefit. What are the consequences of his sin? Now, taking your reading a step further, consider that in the same way Gehazi couldn't deceive Elisha, you can't deceive God. In the light of this fact, how should you live?

Write the theme of chapter 5 on your 2 KINGS AT A GLANCE chart.

DAY SEVEN

Store in your heart: Isaiah 45:22; Proverbs 18:10.

Read and discuss: Deuteronomy 8:11-20; 1 Kings 22:51-53; and 2 Kings 1:1-18.

QUESTIONS FOR DISCUSSION OR INDIVIDUAL STUDY

- ∞ What were the conditions God set forth in Deuteronomy concerning serving other gods?

- ∞ Why is idol worship such a critical issue with God?

- ∞ Where did Ahaziah's power come from?

- ∞ Read 1 Kings 22:51-53 and review the description of Ahaziah. Was he a worshiper of God?

- ∞ According to 2 Kings 1:1,2, from whom did Ahaziah seek wisdom concerning his sickness?

- ∞ What were the results of this search?

- ∞ From whom do you seek wisdom when you have questions about your future?

   a. Do you read your horoscope? Do you ever seek information or counsel from a medium, fortune-teller, or telephone psychic—even if it's just for fun or curiosity?

   b. Whom or what should you seek if you are going to please God? Have you thought about the fact that we serve a living God who is concerned about our daily needs and circumstances? His desire is for us to seek Him when we have questions; therefore, we need to ask ourselves if we are turning to God *before* we turn to anyone else in our quest for answers to life's problems. Where do you run in times of trouble? Whose word can you trust?

THOUGHT FOR THE WEEK

In the days of Elisha, God used prophets to proclaim His plans to the people so they might heed the word of the Lord. The kings were also subject to the same order. When a king wanted God's wisdom, he often sought God's counsel through a prophet.

However, in our time, because of our justification through the blood of Jesus and because of Jesus Christ's resurrection from the dead, there is no longer the need to communicate with God through a prophet. The veil that hung in the temple separating man from God was rent in two the moment Jesus died. Jesus now sits at the right hand of the Father, ever living to make intercession for us. And because the veil of the flesh of the Son of God has been torn in two, we now have direct and open access to the Father through the Son. To take advantage of this access means to live in constant communion and intimacy with the Sovereign Ruler not only of the universe, but also of our world.

You have Jesus, and you have the completed Word of God. How God longs to communicate His heart directly to you—to have you know Him and to walk in His ways. This is why you have something better than human prophets. You have all the wisdom of God recorded and preserved for you in the Bible.

Thus the question becomes, Are you listening to Him or are you seeking counsel like Ahaziah did from gods who are not the true and living God? Are you listening to prophets who give you chaff—their visions, dreams, and prophecies—or are you doing as Elijah admonished Ahaziah? Are you inquiring of "God's Word"? Remember, it will always be "according to the word of the Lord."

So many people today are so quick to run to a new dream, prophecy, vision, or revelation and so negligent to give the necessary diligence required to know the Word of God (the Bible) for themselves. Consequently, many in the body of Christ find themselves tossed to and fro by every wind of doctrine and cunning craftiness of man. They are led astray because they do not come to God His way. God, in these last days, has spoken to us through His Son. May we pay close attention to what He has said.

O Beloved, you know where He is. You are learning who He is. Now order your life accordingly; obey every word that proceeds out of the mouth of God.

HAVE YOU DESTROYED THE HIGH PLACES OF YOUR PAST?

ᗡᗡᗡᗡ

By now it's apparent that the majority of Israel and Judah's kings were wicked. We hope you have seen the repeated statement, the kings "did evil in the sight of the LORD, and were not careful to walk in the ways of the LORD." The kings did evil because they resorted to the high places, rather than to God.

As you do this week's study, ask God to show you any "high places" you have erected in your own life—places, things, and people who have usurped God.

DAY ONE

This week, if you carefully observe all that God does, you will see the extent of His sovereignty, and, as you see this, your respect for Him should reach an even greater depth of appreciation and trust.

Read 2 Kings 6 and mark the key words. Also, in a specific color mark the prophecies given by Elisha, as well as their fulfillments.

Make additions to your list on Elisha. Don't forget to note the miracles wrought by him. Also add new insights to your key words lists.

Over and over in 1 and 2 Kings we are reminded that God is sovereign. It is He who delivered the people from the king of Aram—not Elisha or Israel. It is He who provided the army of angels and struck the Aramean army with blindness. Have you thought, Beloved, of the load, the burden, that could be lifted from your shoulders once you really know and understand the fact that ultimately God is in total control of all the circumstances of our lives? Nothing can transpire without His knowledge or permission. Will this make a difference in how you deal with life's events?

Identify and record the theme of chapter 6 on the 2 KINGS AT A GLANCE chart.

DAY TWO

Read and mark 2 Kings 7. Continue compiling your list on Elisha and the miracles God performs through him.

In the first verse, Elisha gives a word from the Lord concerning Samaria. Be sure to mark the prophecy and its fulfillment in your special color. When God says something, He stands by His word!

After discerning the chapter theme, record it on the AT A GLANCE chart.

DAY THREE

Read 2 Kings 8. Mark the key words, time phrases, and geographical locations.

On the map on the next page note any locations you have marked in the text.

Add to your list on Elisha. Then record on your KINGS OF ISRAEL AND JUDAH chart what you learn about the

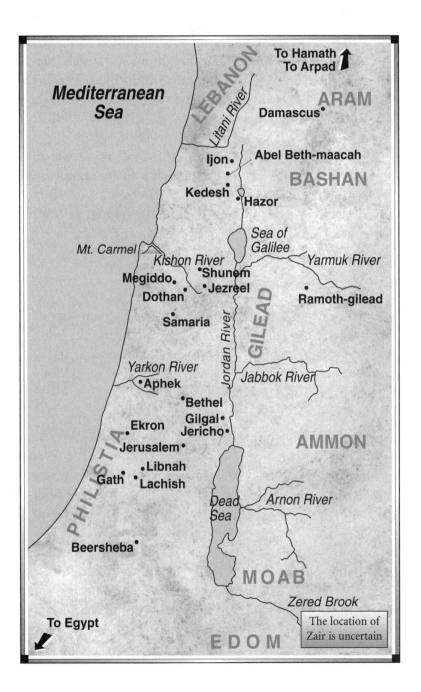

Mediterranean
Sea

LEBANON

To Hamath
To Arpad

ARAM

Litani River

Damascus •

Ijon •

Abel Beth-maacah

BASHAN

Kedesh •

Hazor •

Sea of
Galilee

Yarmuk River

Mt. Carmel

Kishon River

Shunem •

Megiddo •

Jezreel •

Ramoth-gilead •

Dothan •

Samaria •

GILEAD

Jordan River

Yarkon River

Aphek •

Jabbok River

Bethel •

Ekron •

Gilgal •

Jericho •

Jerusalem •

AMMON

Gath •

Libnah •

Lachish •

Dead
Sea

Arnon River

Beersheba •

MOAB

Zered Brook

To Egypt

EDOM

The location of
Zair is uncertain

following kings: Joram (Ahab's son), Jehoram (Jehosha-phat's son), and Ahaziah. (This is a different Ahaziah than the previous one, so note it carefully.) If the lifestyle of the king is described, whether righteous or wicked, color-code it as you have done before, and mark which kingdom he rules.

When you finish charting this information, review all you have compiled about the kings up to this point on THE KINGS OF ISRAEL AND JUDAH chart.

Also, review the information you've written in your notebook concerning the prophets Elijah and Elisha.

DAY FOUR

Today read 2 Chronicles 21 and follow the same mark-ing procedures you've been using. Watch carefully what God does. Think about how this shows His sovereignty.

Mark and chart the relevant information concerning the kings, and add to your key words list.

DAY FIVE

Read 2 Kings 9 and 2 Chronicles 22:1-9. Mark the key words, time references, and geographical locations in both of these passages. Add any new insights you discover on Elisha to your list.

Chart the relevant information concerning Ahaziah and Jehu. Mark their kingdoms and color-code their lifestyles as you have on the other kings. In a special way, mark the instructions given to Jehu concerning his king-ship in 2 Kings 9:1-10. Read 1 Kings 21:17-24 as a refresher on the prophecy concerning Ahab and Jezebel. Mark the fulfillment of the prophecy concerning her. Read the parallel passage in 2 Chronicles 22:7-9.

Second Kings 9:29 says Ahaziah became king in the eleventh year of Joram, while 2 Kings 8:25 says he became king in the twelfth year of Joram. Although these differing dates may seem contradictory, they are not. Rather, they reflect two different dating systems. Ahaziah became king in 841 B.C., which, according to the nonaccession-year system, was Joram's twelfth year. However, the accession-year system (which states that the first official regnal year did not begin until New Year's Day of the year following the year when the new king came to the throne) records it as Joram's eleventh year. In 2 Kings 8:25 the nonaccession-year system was used. Second Kings 9:29 uses the accession-year system. By the accession-year system, it was the eleventh year of Joram, but it was the twelfth year by the nonaccession-year system.*

Identify the theme of 2 Kings 9 and record it on the 2 KINGS AT A GLANCE chart.

DAY SIX

Today your assignment is to read and mark 2 Kings 10. Refer back to 1 Kings 21:17-24 and read the prophecy given concerning Ahab's house. Note the fulfillment of this prophecy in 2 Kings 10.

Although Jehu was obedient to God in many key areas, he wasn't in everything. In order to highlight the life of Jehu, mark 2 Kings 10:31 in a special way. Can you see that it isn't enough for us to be obedient in *some* areas of our

---

* Gleason L. Archer, *Encyclopedia of Bible Difficulties* (Grand Rapids, MI: Zondervan Publishing House, 1982), p. 206.

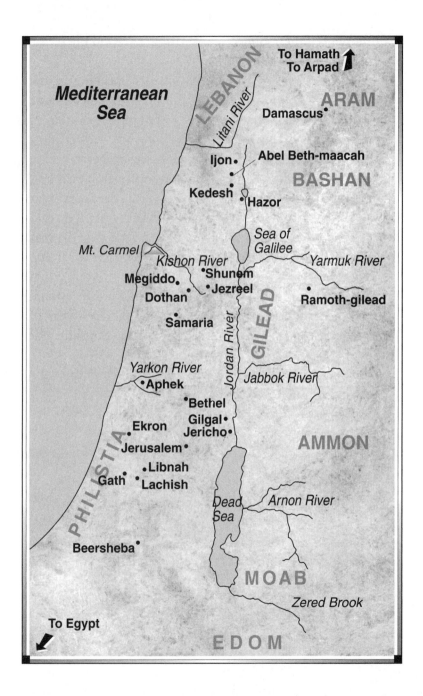

lives? We must walk faithfully in *every* area, serving God with *all* our hearts, bodies, souls, and minds.

Carefully mark the boundaries of Israel in 2 Kings 10:32,33 on the map on the previous page. Why do you think God cut off some of their portions?

DAY SEVEN

Store in your heart: Isaiah 14:27.
Read and discuss: 2 Kings 6:24-33; 7:1-20.

QUESTIONS FOR DISCUSSION OR INDIVIDUAL STUDY

- What was the situation in Samaria according to 2 Kings 6?

- Who did the king blame for this situation?

- What threat did the king of Israel make against Elisha? What do you learn from this regarding threats? Need we fear them? How should we respond? How would your knowledge of God affect your response to threats?

- What prophecy did God give to Elisha concerning Samaria?

- Did God fulfill this prophecy?

- To whom did God first reveal His solution?

- Why do you think the royal officer died?

- What did you learn about God this week? Discuss all the things you saw that God has control over. What does such knowledge mean to you?

THOUGHT FOR THE WEEK

In every situation throughout the period of the kings, God continuously proved Himself to be God and God alone by bringing to pass all of His promises. Yet the people continued to walk in their own ways. They missed the simple truth that it is our responsibility to trust our sovereign God and to live in the light of His promises.

Beloved, as you read these historical chronicles preserved for your learning and admonition, ask yourself if you are living as the children of Israel lived. Are you walking *fully*? Note we said *fully* in the ways of God. Do you live as if what God says is truth and will come to pass?

Since the Garden of Eden, God has proven Himself faithful throughout all generations, yet many people today continue to demonstrate their lack of faith in His character and in His Word by the way they live. O Beloved, let's be careful lest we become like the Israelites, who proved themselves unfaithful even amid God's faithfulness. Let's trust our trustworthy God, our sovereign Lord, and wait patiently on Him as He watches over His Word to perform it (Jeremiah 1:12). For what is written will surely come to pass because it is the Word of God Almighty, the Immutable One!

ARE YOU FOLLOWING IN THE FOOTSTEPS OF YOUR PREDECESSORS OR YOUR KING?

You have probably noticed by now that Israel's success was closely tied to its spiritual condition. When the Israelites were obedient, they prospered; when they walked in their own ways, they experienced defeat.

As you study this week, ask God to show you any areas where you might be tempted to walk independently of Him, so you might not experience defeat but know the spiritual prosperity of obedience.

DAY ONE

Read 2 Kings 11. Mark the key words, time references, and geographical locations.

As you will see, this chapter covers a period of several years in which there was no king over Judah. It will be crucial to your understanding to carefully note all references to time.

Begin a list in your notebook on any information you want to keep on Athaliah (mother of Ahaziah), Jehoiada the priest, and King Jehoash. (His name is spelled *Joash* in 2 Kings 11:2; 12:19,20; 13:1,10; and 2 Chronicles 22:11; 24:1-24; and spelled *Jehoash* in 2 Kings 11:21–12:18.)

Note in 2 Kings 11:4 that another covenant is made binding two parties together under an oath. Then, if you are compiling all you learn from marking the key words, list the covenants made in 2 Kings 11:17-20. Be sure to notice what the people did after the death of Athaliah. Also add to your lists on the key words.

DAY TWO

Your assignment today is to read 2 Chronicles 22:10–23:21, which parallels 2 Kings 11. Look for and note any additional insights not covered in Kings.

Mark and chart the relevant information concerning the kings if you haven't already done so. Record the covenants made in these chapters like you did yesterday.

Identify the themes of 2 Chronicles 22 and 23, and record them on the proper chart.

DAY THREE

Read 2 Kings 12, and mark the key words. Pay special attention to the time phrases because this chapter covers a substantial period.

Build on your lists on (Jehoash) Joash, king of Judah. Color-code the description of each king's lifestyle, and fill in the appropriate information concerning each king on the chart on pages 121-24. Although Joash is described as doing right in the sight of the Lord, note the mistakes he made.

Identify and record the chapter theme on the 2 KINGS AT A GLANCE chart.

DAY FOUR

Read 2 Chronicles 24. As you proceed, mark key words and time phrases. Many of the events in this chapter parallel those in 2 Kings 12, so watch for any additional insights given in 2 Chronicles.

Notice the age of Joash when he became king. Color-code and chart the relevant information concerning him. Note what Joash attempted to do under the influence of Jehoiada. It is interesting to see how Joash was able to stand strong when he had the godly influence of Jehoiada, but what happened when Jehoiada died? Notice what Joash did to Jehoiada's son, Zechariah (vv. 20-22).

DAY FIVE

Read 2 Kings 13 carefully. Mark the key words, time phrases, and geographical locations. As you color-code the kings, be especially careful to observe which king the text is describing. (In 2 Kings 13 both the king of Judah and the king of Israel have the same name, and both names have different spellings.)

Add to your list any new insights on Elisha. After identifying the chapter theme, record it on the appropriate chart. Also add any new information to THE KINGS OF ISRAEL AND JUDAH chart.

DAY SIX

Read 2 Kings 13 again. This time, write down what you learn with respect to the Lord's compassion on His people, even in their disobedience. Watch the closing verses of this chapter. Also note the Lord's faithfulness to His Word, then reflect on His faithfulness to you. Isn't it comforting to know that God remains faithful to His covenant with us?

DAY SEVEN

Store in your heart: Proverbs 3:5,6.
Read and discuss: 2 Chronicles 24.

QUESTIONS FOR DISCUSSION OR INDIVIDUAL STUDY

∾ How old was Joash when he became king?

∾ How did he live in the sight of the Lord? For how long? Did he do what was right in the sight of the Lord?

∾ What significant event happened under Joash? Whose idea was it to restore the house of the Lord? Did he accomplish this work?

∾ What happened when Jehoiada the priest died?

∾ What did they do to Zechariah, Jehoiada's son? Why?

∾ What did God do to Judah as a result?

∾ What did you learn about God this week that you can apply to your life?

THOUGHT FOR THE WEEK

It was evident in the life of Joash, king of Judah, that his commitment to God and his faithful lifestyle were due largely to the influence of the priest Jehoiada. As long as Jehoiada was around, Joash did what was pleasing to God;

when Jehoiada died, Joash turned to the wisdom and counsel of man.

Spiritual mentors—men and women of God we respect, look up to, and imitate, elders and friends who hold us accountable—are part of God's design. However, the help of even godly "flesh" is never to be a substitute for our personal relationship with the living God.

Continue in your study of the Word, Beloved. Determine that you are going to live according to its statutes and precepts. Then your confidence in God will be so strong that you will always fear and obey Him simply because you know who and what He is.

IF GOD IS GOD, WHY DO WE SOMETIMES SERVE HIM HALFHEARTEDLY?

∽∾∽∾

Many times we give God lip service, but our hearts are far from Him. Could part of the reason be that we have never totally forsaken the world's high places—the monuments we serve in order to "make it" in this world? This is the question we must ask as we study the lives of kings and commoners so we will read *and* learn from the lessons God has provided for us.

DAY ONE

Read 2 Kings 14 slowly, marking key words and time phrases. Chart the facts about the following kings: Jehoash, king of Israel; Amaziah, king of Judah; Jeroboam, king of Israel. Review your chart and note that this is the second king of Israel whose name is Jeroboam. Chart the lifestyle of each king and the land he oversees using your usual method of color-coding.

Amaziah is described as doing right in the sight of the Lord in some things but not in all. Thus far, which kings have you seen who were willing to take down the high places? Breaking the chains of idolatry takes effort. Remember that God desires total, not partial, obedience. We are to be obedient in *all* that He commands us.

DAY TWO

Today read the accounts in 2 Chronicles 25 for additional insights into 2 Kings 14. Watch for and color-code additional information concerning the kings, then add it to the chart of the kings.

Identify and record the themes of 2 Kings 14 and 2 Chronicles 25 on the appropriate charts.

DAY THREE

Your assignment today is to read 2 Kings 15, marking key words. We're sure this has become a habit by now! Remember to chart and color-code the information concerning the kings as you encounter them in the text. As you chart each of these kings, try to develop a historical understanding of the progression of the events during their reigns.

Azariah was a righteous king; he did right in the sight of the Lord. But a change came in his heart. Read Proverbs 16:5. Can you identify with giving God some of your life, but not everything? Just remember: He not only wants your all, but, as God, He merits it. How quickly we can forget this if we aren't careful!

DAY FOUR

Read 2 Chronicles 26, continuing to mark key words, time phrases, and geographical locations. The beginning of this chapter talks about Uzziah. It will help you to know that Azariah in 2 Kings and Uzziah in 2 Chronicles are the same person. You will get more details on Azariah (Uzziah) in this chapter which you will want to record. (The very act of writing something out helps you retain it even more. If you also read it aloud, your retention rate will increase even more.)

In this passage, we see that Ahaziah changed. What was that change, and what happened as a result? Note specifically what Azariah (Uzziah) did to be smitten by God. Do you see how seriously God takes sin and the consequences of disobedience? Do you think God's character has changed since the days of the kings? Does God change?

Do you see any LFLs in this chapter to hold in your heart?

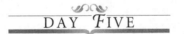

DAY FIVE

Read 2 Chronicles 27, and chart and color-code the information concerning Jotham. Mark key words and time phrases as you study. Notice in verse 6 why Jotham became a mighty king. Isn't it interesting that the kings who were consistently blessed were the ones who followed God?

DAY SIX

Your assignment today is to read 2 Kings 16 and 2 Chronicles 28. Remember to mark key words, time phrases, and geographical locations. Chart and color-code the information on the lifestyle of Ahaz, king of Judah.

Now that you have studied Ahaz, isn't it sad that God once again has a wicked king ruling over His people? In your study today, you will see that many of the events in 2 Chronicles 28 parallel those in 2 Kings 16; however, you will want to look for and record any additional insights in Chronicles that you gain with respect to Ahaz.

Identify and record the chapter themes on the AT A GLANCE charts.

DAY SEVEN

Store in your heart: Psalm 119:105,106 or 2 Chronicles 26:16 (as a reminder to us to beware when we become strong).

Read and discuss: 2 Kings 14:1-29; 2 Chronicles 25.

QUESTIONS FOR DISCUSSION OR INDIVIDUAL STUDY

∾ What did you learn about Amaziah in the opening verses of 2 Kings 14 and 2 Chronicles 25?

∾ What does it mean when 2 Chronicles 25:2 says, "And he did right in the sight of the LORD, yet not with a whole heart"? What did Amaziah do right in this chapter? Why?

∾ Does 2 Kings 14 shed any light on where Amaziah was compromising, where he was not following God with all his heart?

∾ What happened to Amaziah after he defeated Edom? What did Amaziah do to provoke God's anger? How did Jehoash describe him in 2 Kings 14:10 and 2 Chronicles 25:19? What were the consequences of his disobedience?

∾ Did Amaziah turn back to God?

∾ Are you doing right in the sight of the Lord? Discuss what it means to follow after God with a "whole heart"

(Proverbs 3:5,6). What is it today that keeps men and women from following God wholeheartedly? What are some of the issues that you are dealing with? How do you handle these issues…what seems to keep you from dealing with them?

THOUGHT FOR THE WEEK

In 2 Kings 14:3, there is a familiar verse concerning Amaziah. It says, "He did right in the sight of the LORD, yet not like David his father; he did according to all that Joash his father had done."

As you read Kings and Chronicles, it becomes apparent that David set the standard God expected from His kings. Amaziah followed God, but not in everything. The high places were not taken down, which means the people were still sacrificing and burning incense there. Amaziah fell short of the standard set by God's servant David because he did not follow after God with a "whole heart."

Just like Amaziah, Christianity in our world today fails to live according to the standards of holiness as demonstrated in the life of God's Son and as recorded in His Word. God's desire is that His people would be wholly His, totally committed to His will in every circumstance regardless of the personal or physical outcome. Yet many people follow Him halfheartedly. God's desire is that His servants would be people after His own heart as was His servant David. David was a man who did not let his victories or defeats determine the way he lived. Rather, David believed God, took Him at His Word, and pressed on…even like the apostle Paul, forgetting those things which were behind (Philippians 3:13).

Think of the strength and victory multitudes would experience if only they would believe God and behave even as David did, serving Him wholeheartedly! Think of what it could mean for you!

*W*HAT *D*OES *I*T *T*AKE TO *M*AKE *U*S *U*NDERSTAND THE *C*ONSEQUENCES OF *O*UR *S*IN?

As you begin this week, keep in mind what has happened thus far in your study. You have seen a clear picture of the faithfulness of God contrasted with the hardness of man's heart. Perhaps you have already asked, "How long will God allow the people of Israel to walk in their own ways?"

This week you will find the answer to that question.

DAY ONE

Read 2 Kings 17, and mark the key words and time references. Also mark the word *custom(s)*[25] in this chapter, then make a list of what you see concerning custom(s).

In 2 Kings 17, the land of Israel is invaded by Shalmaneser, king of Assyria. Record what you learn about him in your notebook and why he besieged Israel and what he did to the cities of Samaria. Why did God allow this to occur? Could this have been avoided? Look at the map THE ASSYRIAN CAPTIVITY OF ISRAEL on page 88 and the chart ISRAEL'S DIVISION AND CAPTIVITY on page 37 to see the stages of Israel's captivity. Notice when the Assyrian captivity occurred in comparison to the Babylonian captivity, which occurred in three stages.

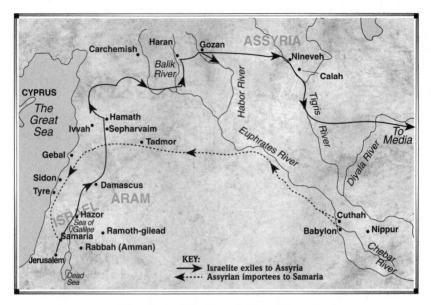

The Assyrian Captivity of Israel

In this chapter, we also see that, although they feared God, the people were worshiping idols in the high places. The people were breaking the covenant they had made with God—to worship and serve Him alone (Deuteronomy 4:23). Think of the generations that were affected by their disobedience.

Make notes on any new insights you glean from marking your key words. Also add Hoshea to your list of kings. Use your color-coding system to differentiate his lifestyle and his kingdom as good or evil. Record any pertinent information you observe about him on your chart.

Identify and record the theme of 2 Kings 17 on the 2 KINGS AT A GLANCE chart.

DAY TWO

Read 2 Kings 18:1-12. Mark key words and references to time. Chart the relevant information on King Hezekiah on your chart and color-code his lifestyle. It would be helpful for you to compile a list of facts on Hezekiah in order to clearly see the kind of king God desired from the beginning.

What difference do you see in Hezekiah in comparison to the other kings who were considered righteous? Why was the king of Assyria able to take Israel captive (2 Kings 18:11,12)? Where was Hezekiah, king of Judah, placing his trust? Was this typical of the kings before him?

DAY THREE

Your assignment today is to read 2 Chronicles 29. Many of the events in this chapter are parallel to those in 2 Kings 18:1-12. Continue your list on Hezekiah as you seek to understand any differences between Hezekiah and the other righteous kings. Notice in verse 3 how quickly Hezekiah began to do the Lord's work.

Add any new insights from marking your key words to your lists. Don't forget to record the chapter theme.

DAY FOUR

Read 2 Chronicles 30, remembering to mark key words and time references as you study. Continue to compile your list on Hezekiah. To what extent did Hezekiah honor God? Note why Hezekiah wanted the people to observe the

Passover. What would be the results if they returned to the Lord? Notice how effective the prayers of the people were and why.

Add additional insights to your key words lists in your notebook.

DAY FIVE

Read 2 Chronicles 31, and mark the key words. The first verse of chapter 31 is an exciting verse. Mark in a significant way what takes place in this verse. Add to your list on Hezekiah, noting what was accomplished as a result of his reign. Record what happens in verse 10 as a result of the obedience of Hezekiah and the people.

Add pertinent insights in your notebook.

DAY SIX

Read 2 Chronicles 31 again today. Read the chapter with the following questions in mind: Why did Hezekiah prosper in all that he did? Do you think it would make a difference today if Israel or the United States had a leader like Hezekiah? It is evident from our study that much rises and falls on leadership! What a good thing to remember! Maybe it would change our sense of responsibility in exercising the privilege given us to elect our leaders.

Record the chapter theme on the AT A GLANCE chart.

DAY SEVEN

Store in your heart: 2 Kings 18:6,7.

Read and discuss: 2 Kings 17:1-18; 18:1-8; 1 Kings 2:1-4; Exodus 20:3-6.

QUESTIONS FOR DISCUSSION OR INDIVIDUAL STUDY

∾ What took place in 2 Kings 17:1-18? How long was Israel besieged? Where were the people of Israel taken?

∾ Were the Israelites given more than one opportunity to turn from their evil ways? How did God warn them? (See 2 Kings 17:13,14.)

∾ Was idol worship the Israelites' only problem? Make a list of their sins (17:15-18).

∾ What punishment did the sons of Israel receive?

∾ Do you think God is serious about His commandment concerning idolatry? (See Exodus 20:3-6.)

∾ Who was the first king since David to tear down the high places?

∾ How many kings reigned in 18:1-8?

∾ Compare and discuss 2 Kings 18:1-8 with 1 Kings 2:1-4.

∾ Was Hezekiah keeping the charge that David gave Solomon?

∾ What can you learn about God from comparing these passages?

∾ Are you, like Hezekiah, obeying God in all that He commands? Discuss.

THOUGHT FOR THE WEEK

Israel is in captivity. Judah is at war. Under the leadership of different kings, Israel and Judah both stepped out of the will of God. The people of God continually served other gods on the high places. They disobeyed God in war and in freedom, and they fought among themselves.

All this was going on when God had clearly promised them success if they would only be strong and courageous and do according to all He commanded them, not turning to the left or to the right.

It is so easy to sit and analyze the history of Israel and the consequences of their response to the clear commandments of God. God not only laid out for them the blessings of obedience but also the very certain consequences of disobedience. As we look at the end result of it all, we wonder why the children of Israel were so foolish to think they could get away with ignoring the commandments of God. Yet what about us? Don't we have a tendency to live the same way? To treat God's commandments lightly, to think we can sin and not pay the consequences, to imagine that as chosen children of God we can escape the just judgment of God? Do we think we are exempt? Do we forget that judgment begins at the house of God?

Romans 15:4 and 1 Corinthians 10 tell us that the things which were written beforehand were written for our example, admonition, encouragement, and perseverance.

O Beloved, may we consider the consequences of our actions before we take them. May we give careful attention to the things we have learned so that they may become an integral part of our lives. May we remember that, as Christians, we have an even greater accountability before God because we are indwelt by the Spirit of God—the very Spirit who promises us victory over the flesh if we will be led by Him.

THE TIME
OF WAR

The Bible says there is no discharge in the time of war (Ecclesiastes 8:8). Do you realize that every day you leave your home you are entering the battlefield? The devil, the prince of this world, has not yet been cast out so it is no wonder that in this world we have tribulation.

When you step into the devil's domain, are you "armed and dangerous," a threat to his kingdom because of your knowledge of the Word? Or are you, like so many, weak and defenseless? It is our prayer that you will arm yourself this week by not entangling yourself with the affairs of this life, but by giving full attention to the Word of God. This enables you to put on the full armor of God so you can stand as more than a conqueror.

DAY ONE

Your assignment today is to read 2 Kings 18:13-37. As you study, mark key words and chart the pertinent information concerning Hezekiah.

When you observe the text, look for the answers to the following questions: Did the Assyrians respect Hezekiah's God? Where was Sennacherib asking them to place their trust? To whom does Sennacherib compare God?

Write the new insights in your notebook. Identify and record the theme of 2 Kings 18 on your 2 KINGS AT A GLANCE chart on page 116.

DAY TWO

Read 2 Chronicles 32:1-23, marking key words, time phrases, and geographical locations. These verses parallel those in 2 Kings 18.

Continue to record your insights on Hezekiah. What is his spiritual condition when Sennacherib invades Judah? Note whether Hezekiah simply trusts God and doesn't do anything or trusts God *in* his preparation. What is Sennacherib's strategy? Note how the Assyrians speak of God in 2 Chronicles 32:19.

DAY THREE

Read 2 Kings 19. Mark the key words and time phrases and add any new insights to the lists you are compiling. Note who fights and wins the battle between Judah and Assyria. Is there any doubt as to who was in control? Meditate on Hezekiah's prayer by noting the main points in his prayer and his motivation for his request. What was the result of Hezekiah's prayer? What is the motivation for your prayers? Think about what you can learn from the way Hezekiah prayed.

DAY FOUR

Read 2 Kings 20, continuing your list on Hezekiah. Note the final events in Hezekiah's life as recorded in this chapter.

Mark the prophecy concerning Judah, and look for its fulfillment as you progress in this week's study.

Identify the chapter theme and record it on the 2 KINGS AT A GLANCE chart.

DAY FIVE

Read the parallel account of Hezekiah's illness in 2 Chronicles 32:24-33, marking the texts and making your lists.

Note why the wrath of God did not come to Jerusalem in the days of Hezekiah.

Chart the information on Hezekiah in the appropriate place.

After discerning the chapter theme, record it on the appropriate chart. Make sure your chapter themes are up to date.

DAY SIX

Read Isaiah 36–39 today. It is a good review of Hezekiah's life. If you gain any new insights, record them on the list you are keeping on Hezekiah. By the way, do you realize how valuable these lists on the kings of Israel and Judah are? Think of all you have seen!

If you have time, reflect on all you have learned about Hezekiah. Think about the difference between Hezekiah and the other "righteous" kings. You might want to reread 2 Kings 18–20 and 2 Chronicles 29–33. Observe how quickly Hezekiah takes his stand. Did he wait to establish himself before he began to make changes? Did he compromise in difficult situations? Where did he turn in difficult times? Think about what principles or precepts you have learned from the life of Hezekiah that you can apply to your own life.

DAY SEVEN

Store in your heart: 2 Chronicles 32:7,8.
    Read and discuss: 2 Chronicles 32:1-23; Isaiah 36–39.

QUESTIONS FOR DISCUSSION OR INDIVIDUAL STUDY

∾ If someone were to ask you what you know about Hezekiah, the king, how would you respond?

∾ Discuss the following statements regarding Hezekiah:

1. The kingdom he ruled over
2. What he did when he took the throne
3. What his reign was like
4. What was significant about his life
5. Who his enemies were
6. What his relationship with God was like

∾ What did you learn about Hezekiah in the verses preceding 2 Chronicles 32?

∾ What was Hezekiah's first response to Sennacherib? Did he put his head in the sand, or did he take the responsibility to prepare for war? What can we learn about our warfare from this example?

- ∽ Why could Hezekiah say, "Be strong and courageous, do not fear or be dismayed because of the king of Assyria" (2 Chronicles 32:7)?

- ∽ Where did Hezekiah place his trust?

- ∽ What were the tactics of Sennacherib? What did he say with respect to God? Discuss Sennacherib's statement in 2 Chronicles 32:14,15.

- ∽ What did God do?

- ∽ What problem did Hezekiah have with his heart? What happened as a result of it? How is this a warning for us? How does this go with the verse you memorized in Week Four—2 Chronicles 26:16?

- ∽ If there is time, discuss any additional insights you gained about Hezekiah from reading Isaiah 36–39.

- ∽ What is the most significant insight you discovered this week that you can apply to your own life? How do you intend to do that?

THOUGHT FOR THE WEEK

Whether your enemies believe it or not, God is God and there is nothing they can do to thwart what He wants to bring to pass. One of the biggest mistakes man can make is to compare and treat the God of Abraham, Isaac, and Jacob as if He were like other so-called gods.

Sennacherib had no respect for the God of Israel because he had seen, through his own experience, that the gods of other people couldn't stop his army. However, when Sennacherib encountered the only living God, he was defenseless and defeated.

Despite all Sennacherib's claims and threats, Hezekiah knew where to turn. It was God who fought the battle because it was His to fight.

Beloved, do you truly believe that the God whom you serve is like no other? Do you realize that He is all-powerful, and no one can defeat Him or thwart what He wants to accomplish? Do you recognize that when God gets involved in a battle, He will win?

Hezekiah's strength was his trust in God. May your strength and confidence be in God. Remember that God rules. No one can stop God from accomplishing His purpose. However, you, like Hezekiah, must do your part. You must be armed and prepared for battle. So keep your sword sharp, valiant warrior, by staying in the Word of God. Keep your heart humble—maintain an attitude of prayer, for God resists the proud, but draws near to the humble...and you do need to be on God's side!

ARE YOU WALKING IN ALL HIS WAYS?

You are walking with God, you are studying the Word of God, but are you walking in *all* His ways?

Israel had been taken captive by the Assyrians; Judah continued to struggle and prosper under the leadership of its kings. Although Hezekiah walked in the ways of the Lord and Judah prospered, he knew he would one day have to pass the scepter of his kingdom to his son. What would that son be like? And what can we learn from his son's life that will help us walk diligently in all God's ways?

DAY ONE

Read 2 Kings 21:1-18. As always, mark key words as you study. Chart any relevant information concerning Manasseh, Hezekiah's son, on THE KINGS OF ISRAEL AND JUDAH chart. Be sure to note whether the lifestyle of Manasseh was evil or good, and color-code the references in your Bible.

Note what God is going to do as a result of the sin of Manasseh and the sin of the people of Judah. You saw last week that God is faithful to His covenant, which means that He must repay Manasseh and Judah for their sin.

DAY TWO

Read 2 Chronicles 33:1-20, and mark the key words. These verses parallel 2 Kings 21:1-18. Continue your list on Manasseh. Record any new insights you gain on him.

When you finish, review all you learned about Manasseh from Kings and Chronicles. Do you see how important it is to compare Scripture with Scripture? If you didn't, you might not be aware of Manasseh's repentance. This is why it is so valuable for you to move through the Bible in this way. Through The New Inductive Study Series you will gain a priceless overview of the *whole* counsel of God.

Such an overview will also keep you from being easily led astray by various winds of doctrine and the craftiness of people who distort the Scriptures. These are critical days, Beloved, and it is imperative that we know the Word of God—it is our plumb line for measuring all that we hear and read.

Record new insights on your key words lists in your notebook.

DAY THREE

Read 2 Kings 21:19-26 and 2 Chronicles 33:21-25. Mark any pertinent key words, then list everything you learn about Amon. Fill in the appropriate information on your KINGS OF ISRAEL AND JUDAH chart.

When you finish, think about these three kings: Hezekiah, Manasseh, and Amon. Compare their lives. These were fathers and sons! Isn't it interesting that even though Hezekiah was one of the godliest kings in the history of

Judah, his son was one of the most wicked? What insight do you gain from that? Is the father always responsible for the way the son turns out? Or does the son bear his own responsibility?

Record the chapter themes.

DAY FOUR

Read 2 Kings 22. Mark the key words and time references. In chapters 22–23 the phrase *the house of the LORD* is very significant. Mark this whole phrase, instead of just the word *house* as you've done previously. Also mark in a distinctive way every reference to *the book,* along with its pronouns. Make a list on what you learn from marking the references to *the book.*

Read Deuteronomy 17:14-20, giving special attention to verses 18-20. Note what the king was to do when he came to power, especially in relationship to the "book of the law." This is the book Josiah found.

Begin a list on King Josiah and color-code the description of his lifestyle. Note carefully what the prophetess tells Josiah and why the Lord God is going to do what He does.

There is so much in 2 Kings 22–23 that is applicable to the church today, for many people have lost the Word of God in the house of God. Think about it.

Identify the chapter theme and record it on your 2 KINGS AT A GLANCE chart and list your information on Josiah on THE KINGS OF ISRAEL AND JUDAH chart.

DAY FIVE

Your assignment today is to read 2 Chronicles 34:1-28. As always, mark the key words, including those you marked

yesterday. Watch the references to time. Look at THE HIS-
TORICAL CHART OF THE KINGS AND PROPHETS OF
ISRAEL AND JUDAH on pages 118-20. Note where Josiah
fits into the chronology of Judah. How close is this to the
approaching Babylonian (Chaldean) captivity? What was it
that Josiah read in the book of the law that caused him
such consternation? One of the things would be the curses
that are recorded in Deuteronomy 28:15-68, especially
verses 36-68. If you read these verses, you will have a better
understanding of Huldah's words to Josiah.

Also, if you have extra study time, it would be profitable to take a good look at the other people mentioned in
this chapter and in 2 Kings 22: Hilkiah the priest, Shaphan
the scribe, and Huldah the prophetess. See what you learn
about each of them. You may want to list your insights in
your notebook.

List any new insights you uncover with respect to
Josiah on your chart.

DAY SIX

Read 2 Kings 23:1-30 and 2 Chronicles 34:29–35:27.
Mark the key words, including those you were told to mark
in 2 Kings 22. Pay close attention to the word *covenant* as
you mark it in these passages.

Mark the references to *Passover*, and make a list of what
you see concerning it.

Remember to continue your list on Josiah and to color-
code his lifestyle. Compare the time phrases you marked in
2 Kings 22:3 and 2 Kings 23:23.

As you read this chapter, note all that was taking place in
relationship to the house of the Lord. If you have *The New
Inductive Study Bible*, look at the two-page, full-color picture

of Solomon's Temple on pages NISB-36 and NISB-37. It will give you a greater appreciation for what you are reading, for this is the house of the Lord that was in such disarray because of the paganism that had crept into Israel's worship.

Identify and record the chapter themes of 2 Chronicles 34–35 on the 2 CHRONICLES AT A GLANCE chart.

DAY SEVEN

Store in your heart: 2 Kings 22:19 or 23:3.

Read and discuss: 2 Kings 22:8-20; 23:1-27; Deuteronomy 17:18-20; 28:64-68.

QUESTIONS FOR DISCUSSION OR INDIVIDUAL STUDY

∿ Describe the situation in Judah and Jerusalem during the days of Josiah.

∿ What turned the situation around in the Southern Kingdom?

   a. What did Josiah read in the book of the law that caused him such anguish?

   b. Why was the king to have his own copy of the law? (See Deuteronomy 17:18-20.)

   c. Discuss the order of events and what the king and the people did.

∿ What was God's message to Josiah through the prophetess Huldah?

∿ What restrained God's hand of judgment upon Judah?

ം What were some of the changes that Josiah made in Judah? What does this tell you about the spiritual condition of the people? How does this compare with the status of some of the churches today?

ം How would you describe the walk of Josiah? If there is time, discuss the action that was taken in chapter 23 on the part of the king and the people.

ം What LFLs did you see in the account of Josiah that could be applied to the church today?

ം From what you have studied, how important is the Word of God for the health of God's people and the society in which we live?

THOUGHT FOR THE WEEK

The Word of God had gotten lost in the house of God. There is no greater illustration, no clearer parallel of what has happened in the church in today's society. The consequences of worshiping God apart from the Word of God was blatantly evident in the decadence of the worship and the worshipers as described in 2 Kings 23—a decadence seen in the state of the church in much of our world today. We have redefined sin and found ourselves tolerating things that God calls abominable. We have, as the Scriptures say, called good evil and evil good. We are a people whose conscience has been seared by the branding iron of iniquity.

And what is our hope? Or is all lost? Our hope—our only hope—is to find the Word of God that is lost in the house of God and return it to its proper place. The church could do nothing greater than to give the Word of God priority in all its activities and to use it as a plumb line for everything it teaches regarding prayer, worship, and every other aspect of Christian life.

It is time for us to humble ourselves before the Lord—to tear our clothes, rend our hearts, and weep before Him. It is time to make a covenant that we will walk after the Lord. We will keep His commandments and His testimonies and His statutes with all our hearts and all our souls, and carry out the word of the covenant by walking in obedience to the indwelling Holy Spirit of God.

It is time for us to let the Word of God dwell richly in our human temples, our bodies, which have been bought with a price. It is time for us to untangle ourselves from the affairs of this life so that we will take time for the Word of God, the daily bread by which we are to live.

This, Beloved, is something that can start with one individual, even as it did with Josiah. Study history. It was individuals who changed the course of history. May you be used to change the course of the church and turn it back to the Word and to holiness.

WHAT DOES IT TAKE FOR GOD TO GET OUR ATTENTION?

God wants our attention—and whatever it takes to get through to us...He will have it!

DAY ONE

Today will serve as a review of how far Israel had come since anointing David as its king. Read 1 Kings 2:2-4, which records David's charge to Solomon. Then read 1 Kings 9:1-9 and 1 Kings 11:1-13. Note the rewards to Israel if they were obedient and the consequences if they were disobedient.

As you studied Kings and Chronicles, did you see any connection or similarities between the lifestyle of the king and the lifestyle of the people? Write out your insights in your notebook.

DAY TWO

Reread 2 Kings 23. In review of last week, were the deeds of Josiah good enough to appease the forthcoming judgment and holy wrath of God? Why? In this chapter, what were God's promises concerning the future of Israel and Judah?

Record on your chart of the kings what you learn concerning Jehoahaz and Jehoiakim.

DAY THREE

Read 2 Kings 24. Mark key words and time phrases. Also observe geographical locations. Consult the following map, EXILES OF JUDAH TO BABYLON. Babylon is modern-day Iraq.

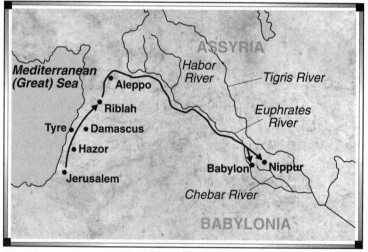

Exiles of Judah to Babylon

Chart the information on the following kings on THE KINGS OF ISRAEL AND JUDAH chart: Jehoiakim, Jehoiachin, and Zedekiah. Also color-code their lifestyles in your Bible.

Begin a list on Nebuchadnezzar, king of Babylon, noting what he does to Jerusalem and the house of God. Refer to the chart ISRAEL'S DIVISION AND CAPTIVITY (page 37), and note the three sieges of Nebuchadnezzar (Babylonian).

Add to your key words lists, and identify and record the chapter theme on the 2 KINGS AT A GLANCE chart.

DAY FOUR

Read 2 Chronicles 36, the parallel account of 2 Kings 24. As you read this chapter and mark key words, don't forget to mark every reference to the *house of the LORD*.

This chapter gives you a good description of the state of the people. Observe it carefully.

When you come to verses 20 and 21, cross-reference them with Leviticus 25:1-5 and 26:34,35. Then when you read verses 22 and 23 in Chronicles, cross-reference them with Jeremiah 25:1-12 and 29:10,11.

Continue to chart the pertinent information on Joahaz, Jehoiachin, and Zedekiah.

DAY FIVE

Read 2 Kings 25, and mark the key words, including every reference to *the house of the LORD*. Note all that happens to the house of the Lord and to the city of Jerusalem.

INSIGHT

As you marked the time phrases, you may have noticed that 2 Kings 24:8 records Jehoiachin as being 18 years old when he began to reign, and 2 Chronicles 36:9 records his age as 8 years old when he began to reign. Since a different age is recorded in the 2 Kings account, general agreement is that there may have been a textual error by the copyist of Chronicles. The 2 Kings account of his age is believed to be more accurate because he is described as "doing evil in the sight of the LORD," and the Babylonians treated him as an adult, not a child. God's Word is inerrant in its original manuscripts; the fact that reconciling these two accounts requires the assumption of a textual error by the copyist in no way takes away from the authority of the Word. A study of the Hebrew numerical system used in Jehoiachin's time reveals how easy it would be for the copyist to fail to properly identify 18 rather than 8 years old.

Complete your chart on Jehoiachin and Zedekiah. Add any new insights to your list on Nebuchadnezzar, and add to your key words lists. Make a special note of what happened to the people of Judah and the house of the Lord. Review the chapters you studied earlier in the week to refresh your memory on the prophecies given. Then look for any account of the fulfillment of these prophecies that were given regarding Jerusalem, the house of the Lord, and the people. You might want to color the fulfillments in a way that matches the prophecies.

Identify and record the theme of 2 Kings 25 on the 2 KINGS AT A GLANCE chart.

DAY SIX

Begin your study by reading 2 Kings 17:1-18. Make a list of the reasons why God allowed Israel to be taken into captivity. Now read 2 Kings 24:1-7, and record the reasons why Judah was taken into captivity. Should this have come as a surprise to Judah? Read 1 Kings 9:1-9 for the answer to this question. God always comes through on His promises—even those which promise a just judgment for disobedience.

DAY SEVEN

Store in your heart: Joshua 1:8.

Read and discuss: 2 Kings 25; 2 Chronicles 36:11-23; Leviticus 25:1-5; 26:27,28,33-35.

QUESTIONS FOR DISCUSSION OR INDIVIDUAL STUDY

ᙣ In what year was Jerusalem finally destroyed by Nebuchadnezzar? (This date is one you should memorize because it's very significant. The information is on the chart ISRAEL'S DIVISION AND CAPTIVITY on page 37.)

∾ When was the Northern Kingdom of Israel taken into captivity? (Again, consult the chart on page 37.)

∾ Discuss why the Southern Kingdom of Judah went into captivity, who took them into captivity, and how long the captivity was to last and why. Discuss Leviticus 25:1-5; 26:27,28,33-35.

∾ What did you learn from 2 Chronicles about the state of the kingdom at the time of Nebuchadnezzar's final siege?

∾ What happened to Jerusalem and the house of the Lord?

∾ How do the accounts of 2 Kings and 2 Chronicles end?

∾ Discuss the differences in the way 2 Kings ends and 2 Chronicles ends. As you discuss 2 Chronicles, compare this with Jeremiah 25:1-12; 29:10,11.

∾ What are the greatest lessons you've learned from this study concerning: God, Israel and Judah, the kings...or a particular king? Record them in your notebook.

∾ What is the most significant lesson you've learned for your own life?

∾ What effect has this type of study had on your life?

THOUGHT FOR THE WEEK

God wanted a people who would follow Him—who would demonstrate on earth the reality of a God who dwells in heaven. So He called Abraham and set aside for Himself a peculiar people, a people of His own possession. People He would redeem from Egypt and bring into a land of their own, a land flowing with milk and honey. He promised to be with them, to guide and watch over them— even though, because of their unbelief, it took 40 years for them to reach the Promised Land, the land He gave to Abraham, Isaac, and Jacob for an everlasting possession.

It wasn't long before His chosen people rejected His rule and asked for an earthly king. God gave them their preference in Saul. Yet, God appointed another, David, a king who He would say was a man after His own heart. The house of David would never lack a man to sit on the throne.

Thus, when David died, Solomon took the throne and began a legacy that would continue for generations. Nearing death, David solemnly charged his son Solomon "to walk in His ways, to keep His statutes, His commandments, His ordinances, and His testimonies, according to what is written in the Law of Moses, that you may succeed in all that you do and wherever you turn, so that the LORD may carry out His promise" (1 Kings 2:3,4).

For a while Solomon did that, and he built the house of the Lord. Yet Solomon disobeyed the clear word of God and multiplied to himself wives from the nations about him. His many wives turned his heart from following God. Consequently, God tore the kingdom in two, and many followed Solomon's ways in worshiping other gods. Far and away, the majority of the kings who would sit on the thrones of this divided kingdom were characterized as doing evil in the sight of the Lord and walking in the way of "their fathers" rather than in the way of "the Father."

Yet a merciful and longsuffering God continued to be gracious to His people, giving them opportunity after opportunity to repent, to return to Him. But they spurned His prophets and stiffened their necks, refusing to believe that the curses recorded in Deuteronomy, in the book of the law, would surely come to pass.

God had to be true to His character; He had to stand by His Word. His Word could not . . . would not be altered. All day long, day in and day out, He stretched out His hands to a disobedient and rebellious people . . . until finally it was over. Done. The Almighty brought down the hammer of the Chaldeans, crushed His holy people that were destroying His city and His sanctuary. They would pay their debt for the land in full. They owed Him seventy Sabbaths; their captivity would last seventy years from 605 B.C. to 536 B.C.

In Kings and Chronicles we find many lessons for life for those upon whom the end of the ages has come. How we pray that we will learn these lessons...and live accordingly.

Like King Josiah of old, may we find *The Book*, read it, and turn to the Lord with *all* our heart and with *all* our soul and with *all* our might, according to *all* the law of Moses....May we fulfill His holy law by walking in the Spirit and setting our minds and affections on things above rather than of this earth.

Theme of 1 Kings:

SEGMENT DIVISIONS

		CHAPTER THEMES
		1
		2
		3
		4
		5
		6
		7
		8
		9
		10
		11
		12
		13
		14
		15
		16
		17
		18
		19
		20
		21
		22

Author:

Historical Setting:

Purpose:

Key Words:

2 Kings at a Glance

Theme of 2 Kings:

Author:

SEGMENT DIVISIONS

Historical Setting:

Purpose:

Key Words:

		CHAPTER THEMES
		1
		2
		3
		4
		5
		6
		7
		8
		9
		10
		11
		12
		13
		14
		15
		16
		17
		18
		19
		20
		21
		22
		23
		24
		25

Theme of 2 Chronicles:

Segment Divisions

			Chapter Themes	Author:
			1	
			2	Historical
			3	Setting:
			4	
			5	
			6	
			7	Purpose:
			8	
			9	
			10	
			11	Key Words:
			12	
			13	
			14	
			15	
			16	
			17	
			18	
			19	
			20	
			21	
			22	
			23	
			24	
			25	
			26	
			27	
			28	
			29	
			30	
			31	
			32	
			33	
			34	
			35	
			36	

THE HISTORICAL CHART OF THE KINGS AND PROPHETS OF ISRAEL AND JUDAH

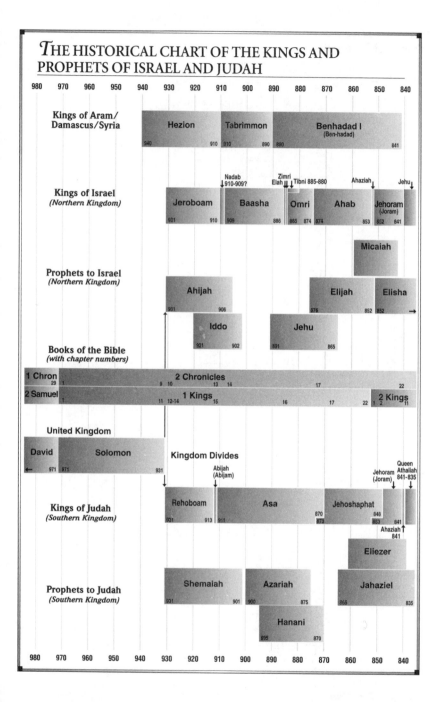

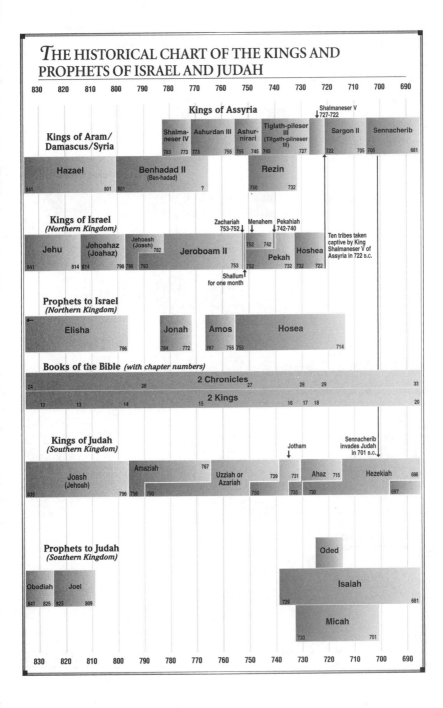

THE HISTORICAL CHART OF THE KINGS AND PROPHETS OF ISRAEL AND JUDAH

THE HISTORICAL CHART OF THE KINGS AND PROPHETS OF ISRAEL AND JUDAH

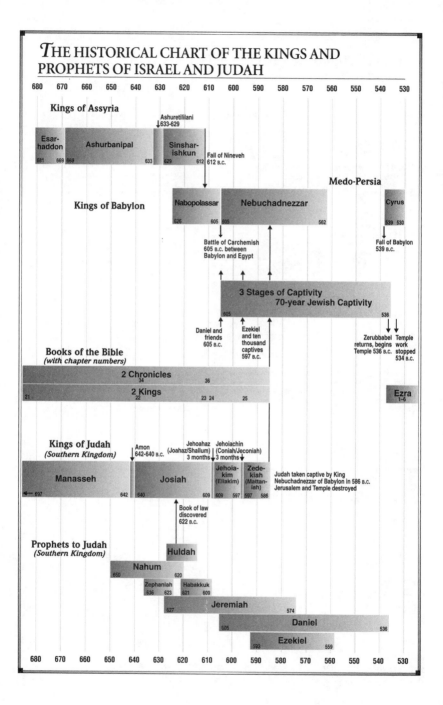

680   670   660   650   640   630   620   610   600   590   580   570   560   550   540   530

Kings of Assyria

Ashuretililani
↓633-629

Esar-haddon 681 669
Ashurbanipal 669 633
Sinshar-ishkun 629 612
Fall of Nineveh 612 B.C.

Medo-Persia

Kings of Babylon

Nabopolassar 626 605
Nebuchadnezzar 605 562
Cyrus 539 530

Battle of Carchemish
605 B.C. between
Babylon and Egypt

Fall of Babylon
539 B.C.

3 Stages of Captivity
70-year Jewish Captivity
605   536

Daniel and friends 605 B.C.
Ezekiel and ten thousand captives 597 B.C.

Zerubbabel returns, begins Temple 536 B.C.
Temple work stopped 534 B.C.

Books of the Bible
(with chapter numbers)

2 Chronicles 34 36
2 Kings 21 22 23 24 25

Ezra
1–6

Kings of Judah
(Southern Kingdom)

Amon
642-640 B.C.

Jehoahaz
(Joahaz/Shallum)
3 months

Jehoiachin
(Coniah/Jeconiah)
3 months

Manasseh 697 642
Josiah 640 609
Jehoia-kim (Eliakim) 609 597
Zede-kiah (Mattan-iah) 597 586

Judah taken captive by King Nebuchadnezzar of Babylon in 586 B.C. Jerusalem and Temple destroyed

Book of law discovered 622 B.C.

Prophets to Judah
(Southern Kingdom)

Huldah

Nahum 650 620

Zephaniah 636 623

Habakkuk 621 609

Jeremiah 627 574

Daniel 605 536

Ezekiel 593 559

680   670   660   650   640   630   620   610   600   590   580   570   560   550   540   530

THE KINGS OF ISRAEL AND JUDAH		
King's Name	Length of His Reign	Facts About His Life

THE KINGS OF ISRAEL AND JUDAH		
King's Name	Length of His Reign	Facts About His Life

THE KINGS OF ISRAEL AND JUDAH		
King's Name	Length of His Reign	Facts About His Life

The Kings of Israel and Judah

King's Name	Length of His Reign	Facts About His Life

NOTES

1. NIV: also *hearts, mind, wholeheartedly, again give allegiance, cheer up, led astray, spirit, wholehearted devotion*

2. NIV: also *follow, continue, live, commit, keep*

3. NIV: also *was faithful, committed, continued, followed, persisted*

4. NIV: also *supplications, plea(d)*
   KJV: also *beseech*

5. NIV; NKJV: also *treaty;*
   KJV: also *league*

6. NIV: also *skilled*

7. NIV: also *curses*

8. NIV: also *called down*
   KJV: also *blaspheme*
   NKJV: also *blasphemed, accursed*

9. NIV: also *give orders, have been told, word, demanded, order(ed), commands*
   KJV: also *word, mouth*
   NKJV: also *have been told, word*

10. NIV: *commands*

11. NIV: also *promises*

12. NIV: also *gave;*
    KJV: also *promised*

13. NIV: also *shrines*

14. NIV: also *wrong, wrongdoing, trouble, disaster, bad, harm, wicked;*
    KJV: also *wicked(ness), bad, mischief;*
    NKJV: also *wicked(ness), trouble, calamity*

15. NIV: also *temple, building;*
    KJV: also *temple;*
    NKJV: also *temple, room*

16. NIV: also *caused to commit, done wrong;*
    KJV: also *sinneth*

17. NIV; NKJV: *had committed*

18. NIV: also *Israelite(s)*

19. NIV: also *Yaudi*

20. KJV: also *darkness*

21. KJV: Does not use *when,* only uses *if*

22. NIV spells it both ways in both books.

23. The words *supplication, wisdom,* and *promise* are not used in 2 Kings.

24. NIV: also *as the LORD had said, in accordance with the word of the LORD;*
    KJV: also *according to the saying of the LORD*

25. NIV: also *practices, what...requires;*
    KJV: *statutes, manner(s);*
    NKJV: *statutes, rituals*

Books in the
New Inductive Study Series

ରେ ରେ ରେ ରେ

HARVEST HOUSE BOOKS
BY KAY ARTHUR

∾∾∾∾

God, Are You There?
How to Study Your Bible
Israel, My Beloved
Just a Moment with You, God
Lord, Teach Me to Pray in 28 Days
A Marriage Without Regrets
A Marriage Without Regrets Study Guide
Speak to My Heart, Lord
With an Everlasting Love

Bibles
The New Inductive Study Bible (NASB)

Discover 4 Yourself
Inductive Bible Studies for Kids
How to Study Your Bible for Kids
Lord, Teach Me to Pray for Kids
God's Amazing Creation (Genesis 1–2)
Digging Up the Past (Genesis 3–11)
Abraham—God's Brave Explorer (Genesis 11–25)
Joseph—God's Superhero (Genesis 37–50)
Wrong Way, Jonah! (Jonah)
Jesus in the Spotlight (John 1–11)
Jesus—Awesome Power, Awesome Love (John 11–16)
Jesus—To Eternity and Beyond! (John 17–21)
Boy, Have I Got Problems! (James)
God, What's Your Name?